A CENTURY OF CINEMA IN DORSET

1896 ✸ 1996

PETER DYSON

1st edition published 1996

ISBN 1 898073 11 2

ACKNOWLEDGEMENTS

Sincere appreciation and acknowledgement is made of quotations, articles and other items from the following newspapers and periodicals:

EVENING ECHO, BOURNEMOUTH
DORSET EVENING ECHO, WEYMOUTH
WESTERN GAZETTE, YEOVIL
BRIDPORT NEWS

POOLE ADVERTISER
BLACKMORE VALE MAGAZINE
FREE PORTLAND NEWS

Assistance and information has also been made readily available from the following organizations and sources of reference. I would like to express my thanks to the members of Staff with whom I came into contact during my research.

BLANDFORD MUSEUM
BOURNEMOUTH REFERENCE LIBRARY
BRITISH BROADCASTING CORPORATION
CINEMA EXHIBITOR'S ASSOCIATION
CINEMA THEATRE ASSOCIATION
DORSET COUNTY MUSEUM
DORSET COUNTY RECORD OFFICE
DORCHESTER REFERENCE LIBRARY
FRIENDS OF PORTLAND MUSEUM
GILLINGHAM MUSEUM
IMPERIAL WAR MUSEUM, LONDON
METRO GOLDWYN MAYER CINEMAS

MUSEUM OF THE MOVING IMAGE, LONDON
ODEON CINEMAS
POOLE REFERENCE LIBRARY
ROYAL AIR FORCE MUSEUM, HENDON
SERVICES SOUND AND VISION
    CORPORATION
SHERBORNE MUSEUM
SPRINGBOURNE LIBRARY, BOURNEMOUTH
TITHE BARN MUSEUM, SWANAGE
WEYMOUTH REFERENCE LIBRARY
YEOVIL REFERENCE LIBRARY

Assistance with photographs kindly given by:
F Crescioli, P Foreman, C Fowler, G Hooper, D Haysom, R Hickson, R Humphires, H Mears, G Slade and Sandford Holiday Park

Many other people throughout Dorset have assisted in this project, as it is impossible to list them all I hope that those I have missed will accept our sincere thanks and appreciation. My wife Pat, has been very supportive and given me valuable help in so many ways also my sister-in-law, Gwen Standfield who patiently and efficiently arranged and typed the original manuscript and lastly our son Ron who painted the cover watercolour.

Publishers note

Power Publications
Ferndown, Dorset

Facing page: *American built "Optigraph" projector*
Front cover: *Regent Theatre, Poole 1953*
Layout: *Mike Power*
Printed by: *Pardy & Sons (Printers) Ltd*

INTRODUCTION

Many books have been written on the County of Dorset covering a wide range of subjects relating to the history and life in the County over many centuries. My aim in these pages is to put on record and give a general picture of a form of entertainment which virtually arrived in Dorset commercially at the beginning of the 20th century.

During the 1890's much experimentation was taking place with cinematography and on the 20 February 1896 Frenchmen Louis and Auguste Lumiere were able to present in London at the Marlborough Hall, Regent Street, a film programme which attracted much public attention. Within a few weeks the same programme was being presented at the Empire Music Hall in Leicester Square, as a twenty minute attraction on the bill.

This was really the beginning of commercial cinema presentation in Britain and venues quickly appeared in London and the major provincial cities and by the turn of the century many smaller towns were beginning to go to the pictures.

It is now something like 100 years since moving pictures put in an appearance in Dorset and my intention is to give a flavour of the exhibiting of films within the County, whether it was in cinemas as we know them or in improvised conditions, village halls, converted chapels and any other available premises in the smaller communities of the County. I have found during my research that much ingenuity was used to bring the early film shows and the later "talkies" to some of the remote rural areas.

Bearing in mind that communications and transport facilities in these areas was virtually non existent in the first quarter of this century, had it not been for some enterprising local tradesmen or business people inhabitants of such areas would have had little opportunity to see the latest products of British and American film studios. Interestingly one of the earliest Dorset village film shows on record is given in the Bere Regis parish magazine in 1903 when a certain Mr Baker from Salisbury gave "An exhibition of cinematograph pictures of the Coronation, seaside scenes and views of foreign countries, diversified with musical performances on a phonograph". This gives some idea of the things that were happening in the villages in the way of popular entertainment. On 14 October 1896 an entertainer billed as Hercat presented "The Cinematographe – Life-size, living moving pictures" at the Shaftesbury Hall (later West's Pictures) in Old Christchurch Road, Bournemouth.

The following month the Theatrograph moving picture show was presented at the Amity Hall Poole on the 13/14 November and the same programme was shown at the Theatre Royal, Bournemouth one week later.

Exactly which was the earliest public film show in Dorset depends on how you view the fact that at this time Poole was in Dorset and Bournemouth was then in Hampshire.

It is likely that the first films seen by the population at large were those provided by travelling showmen who often had a "Bioscope Booth" as part of their fairground attractions. There is certainly evidence that Bioscope shows put in an appearance at Sherborne's Pack Monday Fair at the turn of the century, which would indicate that as they moved around Dorset during their touring season people would have been able to see moving pictures for the first time.

Many of the early town cinemas were located in converted halls and other buildings that lent themselves to such use, and then as entertainment in this field expanded and became more sophisticated the proprietors moved to purpose built cinemas and as the industry moved into the "Talkie" era of the late 1920's most small towns had their own cinema. The majority of Dorset's small town cinemas have gradually disappeared in the last 25 years or so, although it is pleasant to record that the towns of Bridport, Dorchester, Weymouth, Lyme Regis and Wareham still retain their original silver screens and it is nice to know that if plans materialise the Tivoli at Wimborne will be showing films again in 1995 as part of proposals to use this cinema as a multi-purpose entertainment centre.

I do not intend to dwell on too much technical detail of the cinemas as my primary aim is to give an idea of the individual buildings, the people who ran the businesses and some of the people who worked in the industry locally.

It should be explained that some of the older cinemas mentioned in Bournemouth and Christchurch have never really existed within the county of Dorset. This situation was brought about by county boundary changes made in 1974. These changes brought Bournemouth and Christchurch into Dorset. In the interests of giving a reasonably complete record I have included all cinemas that have ever existed within the boundaries of the present day Dorset.

I would like the following pages to be considered a form of tribute to the early pioneers of cinematography both in respect of those who experimented and produced the early cameras and films and to the industry which gradually formed to distribute and exhibit the pictures of those early years, with particular emphasis on such activities in the towns and villages of Dorset.

I have included a section dealing with cinemas on the various Service establishments. There was a Garrison Theatre at Bovington from the time of the First World War and during the Second World War the R.A.F. Station at Warmwell had a cinema and the building, which still exists today, is currently used as the village hall at Crossways. This is quite interesting as very little still remains of this Battle of Britain airfield at Warmwell.

During my research I have met many people who have been pleased to talk of times spent either working or as patrons of their local cinema, whether it was the once weekly show in the humble village hall or the Westover Super Cinema in Bournemouth.

I am very appreciative of their interest and help and I hope that this record will cause cinemagoers throughout Dorset and beyond to remember happy days and nights at their local cinema.

Dorset is my home county and in the course of this research my wife and I have had the opportunity of visiting many corners of the County, some of which we have not seen for many years and others that we never knew existed. My wife Pat shares my interest in "cinema" which began for us when we met whilst we were both working at the Regent Theatre, Poole. My thanks go to her for her patience and help in so many ways during the research and preparation of this review of Dorset Cinemas.

Every effort has been made to cover all known cinemas, although in some instances exact first hand information has been difficult to come by due to the fact that some of the early cinemas were small and very improvised and few records exist of those early days.

Moving into the 1920's and later many people can recall their local cinema and the films that were shown but locating the proprietors and those who worked in the smaller town cinemas has been no easy task. In some cases it has been impossible to obtain first hand information but hopefully some idea has been given of each and every cinema.

Regarding the mobile cinemas and the shows that were provided in the country districts, research has shown that this was a very active field, particularly in the 1920's and 1930's. Many mobile cinema operators existed in the county and few villages or small communities failed to see film shows from time to time. Bearing this in mind it has been impossible to detail each and every operator and all the villages that were served, but an effort has been made to give a flavour of the diversity and type of entertainment that was provided by Dorset's mobile silver screen.

Hopefully the cinemas that have survived the onslaught of television, video and the rest will continue to provide big screen entertainment for many years to come.

On the brighter side it is nice to see that the Tivoli at Wimborne is back in business and in the summer of 1995 a trial run of a drive-in cinema overlooking the sea on the cliffs at Boscombe has been made, and it is hoped that regular shows will begin in July or August either at the Boscombe location or possibly on a larger site in Kings Park.

This has been a summary of Dorset cinema activity from its beginning in 1896 up until the present day.

Some of the photographs which have been included are not exactly first class but in many cases are the only examples showing particular cinemas and equipment. Some were taken with very basic cameras and the negatives have not survived the years.

Such photographs from various sources have never been previously published and hopefully help to provide an interesting record of Dorset's Cinemas in the Twentieth Century.

In conclusion it must be said that researching and compiling this brief record of cinema activities within Dorset has given considerable pleasure.

Now, let's go to the pictures!

PETER DYSON
WIMBORNE 1995

CONTENTS

BLANDFORD

The first moving pictures shown in Blandford were brought by travelling showmen to the Marsh or Fair Field sites just before the First World War.

The earliest cinema was the Electric Picture Palace in East Street. This was in fact the converted cottages adjacent to the White Hart Inn. Proprietors were Messers. Ferrilees of Sherborne.

In 1927 Percival James Carter who had been an entertainer in the music halls in earlier years acquired the Palace and rebuilt the premises in 1929 calling it the New Palace Theatre.

Five years later in 1934 Mr Carter commissioned Bournemouth architect, Mr E. de Wilde-Holding, L.R.I.B.A. to design a new theatre which was duly built on a site virtually opposite, the Old Palace became a shop known as Carter's Bazaar.

In 1940 the Old Palace was reopened as the Ritz mainly to cater for the additional service personnel in the area of Blandford Camp and the R.A.F. Station at Tarrant Rushton.

When very popular films were being shown both cinemas shared the same copy which must have meant smart work by the projectionists and the timing of programmes.

The Ritz closed in 1957. The Kalee '18' projectors and some seating found a new home at the Empire, Wareham (now the Rex).

The Palace closed in 1971 after 37 years as the focal point of local entertainment in Blandford. Closing programme was the feature film version of the television classic DAD's ARMY on 28 August. The building still survives to a large extent, except that internally it has been converted for use as the Gateway Supermarket.

Palace Cinema projection room 1950

Interior of Old Palace Cinema

Palace Cinema, East St. shortly after opening in 1934

BOURNEMOUTH

Bournemouth's steady growth as a leading holiday resort during the Victorian era resulted in every effort being made to provide varied and up to date entertainment for visitors and those taking up residence in the town.

The first recorded public film show in Bournemouth was on 14 October 1896 when the "Cinematographe moving picture show" was screened at the Shaftesbury Hall (later West's Pictures) in Old Christchurch Road.

In November 1896 the Theatre Royal in Albert Road presented the "Theatrograph – Life size moving photographs" for a four week period. The programme was advertised as being direct from the Alhambra Theatre, London.

As far as cinema entertainment was concerned in Bournemouth the "golden age" was probably just prior to the Second World War when the town had 14 cinemas, ranging in size from the Westover in Westover Road with seating for 2600 to the Premier News Theatre in Albert Road which seated just 125 in its original form.

Although much could be written concerning Bournemouth's individual cinemas over the last 90 years it will only be possible in this modest volume to give a general review of cinema activity in the various districts of the town. It must be pointed out that many of the cinemas mentioned in this section have never existed in Dorset due to the fact that until 1974 Bournemouth and Christchurch were part of the county of Hampshire. In order to make a fairly complete record the earlier cinemas and happenings in Bournemouth had to be mentioned.

Central Bournemouth

In 1901 West's Pictures at the Shaftesbury Hall in Old Christchurch Road were presenting films and live entertainment on a regular basis, although it seems that initially these shows were operated seasonally.

One of the earliest films at West's Pictures was THE UNSEEN WORLD which was advertised as "Now engaging the rapt attention of all in London". Proprietor, Mr T J West announced in August 1904 that West's Pictures would run concurrent film programmes at the Assembly Rooms, Boscombe.

The original West's Pictures occupied the upper portion of the Shaftesbury Hall but in 1936 major alterations and improvements were put in hand and seating capacity was increased from 512 to 932. Mr C H Fowler, who was an assistant architect in the practice of Mr E De Wilde Holding, L.R.I.B.A. recalls that the original screen was in fact painted directly on the wall of the auditorium.

After alterations there was access to the new West's Super Cinema from both Old Christchurch Road and St Peter's Road.

The grand re-opening of the cinema was on Whit Monday 1936 when the presentations were LAST DAYS OF POMPEII and Joe E Brown in FUNNYFACE.

Wests continued in business until the air raid on 23 May 1943 when the building was destroyed by a direct hit. The last programme at West's Super Cinema on Saturday, 22 May 1943 was ironically a film entitled THE MORTAL STORM starring James Stewart.

The cinema was never rebuilt and the site is now occupied by shops and the Burlington Arcade in Old Christchurch Road.

In 1904 when Dan Godfrey was arranging and directing programmes in the original Winter Gardens short interludes of films were included in some presentations.

The Bournemouth Daily Echo in March 1904 announced a concert featuring Animated Photos by Raymond's "Vivagraph" Many of the films presented in this venue concerned travel subjects and were shown when visiting lecturers were on the programme. The Winter Gardens in May 1912 was presenting THE TITANIC DISASTER on the Chrono Bioscope - in sixteen scenes.

West's Pictures, Old Christchurch Road, Bournemouth shortly after alterations in 1936

The original Winter Gardens, Bournemouth

The Theatre Royal in Albert Road was also offering bioscope films at this time and special afternoon matinees known as Bioscope Teas. Messrs. Brights departmental store in Old Christchurch Road were keeping up to date in 1912 and advertising "High Class Cinematograph Teas" in their restaurant.

In 1910 Mr William Langley-Taylor and a group of friends purchased 25 and 27 Commercial Road and the premises were converted into the Electric Theatre which operated under the direction of James Bravery and the Popular Bioscope Syndicate of London until 1921.

Due to increased demand for cinema entertainment it was decided to rebuild the theatre and as a result the new Electric opened its doors on 22 December 1921 under the control of Capital and Counties Electric Theatres Ltd. The Mayor of Bournemouth, Alderman C H Cartwright presided over the ceremony which gave central Bournemouth the most comfortable cinema to date. The new building seated 1400 and was designed by leading theatre architects, Messrs. Frank Matchan and Co. who were responsible for designing such theatres as the London Palladium and the Victoria Palace. The Electric had an attractive cafe where it was possible to order teas to be served in the interval and specially adapted trays were provided to clip on the seats in the auditorium. During the 1920's in the "silent" era the Electric boasted a fine 15 piece orchestra conducted by Mr A C Ronald to accompany epics starring Mary Pickford, Charles Chaplin, Rudolph Valentino and many others.

In 1930 the Electric underwent further modernisation and improvements including the installation of a Christie theatre organ with "Radiotone" attachment and the latest Western Electric Sound System for the newly arrived "talkies" The Christie organ remained in regular use until 1954.

The Electric continued to entertain Bournemouth's cinema-goers until 1966 when the last film screened was THE HALLELUJAH TRAIL on 2 March 1966.

Many local people had an affection for the Electric as the programmes were usually good and the cinema comfortable and welcoming. The only people who were not quite so happy were the projectionists who had to cope with cramped and hot conditions in a very small projection room.

Interior of the Electric Theatre shortly after re-opening in 1931

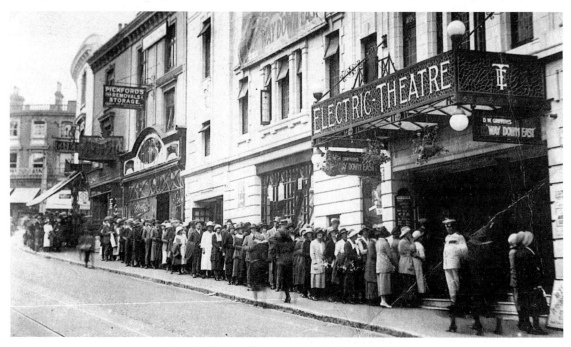

Electric Theatre, Bournemouth in the early 1920's

During the summer of 1910 the Empire Electric Theatre in The Square also began showing films. This picture theatre was situated in Bourne Avenue between the old Swiss Restaurant and the Braidley Road junction. The speciality at the Empire Electric was films taken locally in and around Bournemouth. Their advertising at this time proclaimed that they were the only theatre in Bournemouth showing films of local carnivals, fetes and garden parties. Proprietors of the Empire Electric were the Plymouth, Exeter and Bournemouth Bioscopes Ltd.

Empire Electric Theatre, The Square, Bournemouth, opened as a cinema in 1910

Bioscope film shows in central Bournemouth were also being offered at this time in the Lansdowne Picture Theatre at 197 Old Christchurch Road which was a small enterprise and the screen was immediately behind and above when entering from the main road. Shows started here in 1911 and continued until after the First World War.

Cinematograph Entertainment direct from the Polytechnic Regent Street, London was offered in 1910 at the Westover Palace in Westover Road which also housed a tea house, gardens and a roller skating rink. Music was provided by Percy Pearce and his Orchestra who also played at several other theatres in the town and the Ice Rink in Westover Road.

Childrens' special Empire Day matinees at the Original Westover Cinema in the late 1920's

On the 18 June 1937 the Westover Palace closed as a cinema and on a site immediately next door the brand new Westover Super Cinema opened its doors for the first time the following day. Final film at the Westover Palace was THE PLOUGH AND THE STARS starring Barbara Stanwyck.

The grand official opening of the new Westover was performed by the Rt.Hon.The Earl of Malmesbury and the opening programme starred Fred Astaire and Ginger Rogers in SHALL WE DANCE. The theatre organist at the console of the Compton organ on this occasion was Reginald Porter-Brown who during later years often broadcast from the Westover when appearing here as guest organist.

The Associated British Picture Corporation spared no expense in providing Bournemouth with a tasteful and comfortable super cinema with seating for 2600 and a stylish restaurant and balcony cafe. Architect for the Westover was ABC's house architect, Mr W R Glen.

Being one of the Company's premier cinemas special shows and events often took place at the Westover.

Westover Cinema, Bournemouth in 1954

In 1951 when Councillor Harry Mears was President of the Cinematograph Exhibitors Association, their annual conference was held in Bournemouth and the Westover played a significant part in events, particularly on the 31 May when there was the world premiere of a new British musical HAPPY GO LOVELY starring Vera-Ellen and David Niven.

Over thirty stars including guests from Hollywood attended this sparkling occasion which was followed by a Ball at the Pavilion, then a moonlight cruise on the paddle steamer "Lorna Doone" which ended at Poole Quay at 2 a.m. and then an open air film show was presented on the quay - quite a day. Amongst the special guests at this event were Bebe Daniels, Ben Lyon, Googie Withers and veteran music hall artist George Robey.

Also in 1951 there was the United Kingdom premiere of MGM's SHOWBOAT and after the show the Company invited guests on a cruise aboard the "Lorna Doone" which was renamed for the evening "Cotton Blossom" - the name of the showboat in the film.

Over the years many film celebrities have appeared on stage at the Westover and special shows for charitable organisations have been given, particularly during the period of the Second World War.

Auditorium at the ABC Westover

Ron Hickson at the controls in the projection room of the ABC Westover, Bournemouth 1959

In 1970 the Westover was "twinned" and the two auditoria then seated 644 upstairs and 982 on the ground floor. Opening programmes on 13 June 1970 were PAINT YOUR WAGON and ALL THE WAY UP respectively.

The ABC Westover became part of the Cannon Cinema chain in 1973 and the ground floor auditorium was divided giving a total of three screens.

Since 21 May 1992 the cinema has been operating under the banner of the Metro Goldwyn Mayer Company and the current seating accommodation is 652, 585 and 223 respectively.

Number one auditorium has the largest capacity and is equipped for 70mm film presentation which makes it the only cinema venue in Dorset with this capability. In recent years short seasons of 70mm films have been presented by Manager, Mr Roger Marley, which has given film fans in Bournemouth the opportunity to see the "ultimate cinema experience", as this format has sometimes been called.

It is interesting to note that Mr Marley has had many years of experience in the industry having started in 1955 at the Paignton Picture House and subsequently joining ABC in 1965.

Provincial Cinematograph Theatres Ltd. opened the impressive Regent Cinema Theatre in Westover Road on 13 May 1929. The site was previously occupied by Italian style mansions and was virtually opposite the recently opened Pavilion Theatre.

Seating 2300 the Regent was Bournemouth's largest and most luxurious cinema at this time and was designed by Mr W E Trent in association with Bournemouth architects, Seal and Hardy.

Projection room, Regent, Bournemouth,
in the early 1930's

The building was in Italian Renaissance style with arcaded front against white terra-cotta. The large foyer was paved with black and white marble and the ceilings were richly ornamented and coloured. Marble staircases lead to the auditorium and the two restaurants which accommodated 300. The main restaurant had views of the sea and the distant Purbeck Hills. The auditorium was crowned with a large illuminated dome and the walls were adorned with Italian landscape scenes which were individually lit. These scenes were painted by Frank Barnes and similar murals were to be seen in the restaurants.

The Regent was equipped with a large stage and full theatrical facilities including a mighty Wurlitzer theatre organ which was played by many broadcasting organists in the 1930's and 1940's.

The opening programme featured Ronald Colman in TWO LOVERS on the screen whilst on the stage live entertainment was provided, supported by T.S. Clarke-Browne and his Regent Orchestra and Reginald Foort at the Wurlitzer console. Although TWO LOVERS was a silent film it was only a matter of a few months before the Regent was presenting all the latest "talkies", and one of the earliest of these was the musical BROADWAY MELODY.

During the Second World War when many members of the Royal Canadian Air Force were stationed in the town, special late night films were presented after normal evening performances for Service personnel only. The Regent was also often used for instructional films and other Service activities during this period.

The Regent was renamed the Gaumont in 1949 and continued to provide first class entertainment in the town including occasional live shows featuring such stars as Ella Fitzgerald, Dusty Springfield, Victor Borge and Sarah Vaughan. In August 1963 The Beatles took the stage for a week with two shows each night.

Quite apart from these live shows many film stars appeared on stage promoting their latest films. Jean Simmons, Margaret Lockwood, Petula Clarke and Jack Warner were amongst the many celebrities who came to the Regent in the 1950's and 1960's.

In 1968 the Gaumont closed and work was put in hand to "twin" the theatre. The last featured film in the old theatre was HANG 'EM HIGH starring Clint Eastwood. After conversion Gaumont 1 seated 757 and Gaumont 2 1,168. The latest projection and sound equipment was installed and every comfort was provided but the elegance, beauty and atmosphere of the old Regent was gone forever.

The first programme at Gaumont 1 was ICE STATION ZEBRA and at Gaumont 2 the film was MACKENNA'S GOLD when reopening took place on 15 July 1969. Gaumont 1 was fully equipped for the presentation of Cinerama films.

Chief projectionist Joe Heathman, who has been at the Gaumont/Odeon since 1956, has seen service in other Bournemouth cinemas, namely the Savoy and the Astoria, having started his career at the Premier in Albert Road in 1951. During his time at the Gaumont/Odeon he has seen many changes not least the renaming to Odeon in October 1986 and the introduction of five screens in June 1989, and more recently in 1995 the opening of the sixth screen with a charity premiere of LITTLE WOMEN on 23 February 1995.

Gaumont Theatre, Bournemouth, 1954

The original Odeon in Bournemouth seating 2000 and located in Christchurch Road at the Lansdowne opened with a flourish on 7 August 1937, the same year as the Westover.

The first film was HISTORY IS MADE AT NIGHT starring Charles Boyer and Jean Arthur. The Earl of Malmesbury performed the opening ceremony which was preceded by musical entertainment by the Band of H.M.Royal Marines.

Projection room at the Odeon Lansdowne early in the 1940's

Architect for Odeon Theatres, Mr George Coles, F.R.I.B.A. designed the theatre which eventually incorporated shops and flats on either side. The Odeon had an attractive restaurant on the first floor and Mrs Oscar Deutsch designed the decorative scheme throughout the building. Provision was made in the auditorium for a theatre organ but throughout the life of the cinema this was never utilised. Builders of the theatre were local company, W. Hayward and Son (Bournemouth) Ltd.

Mr Maurice de Jong was Manager here during part of the Second World War period when the Odeon was often used for special shows and events relating to the war effort. Typical of such events was in 1940 when a twelve-year old Bournemouth boy who was rescued when the ship taking him to Canada was torpedoed, appeared on stage to receive a copy of the Movietone newsreel showing his arrival back in Britain.

Also in 1940 on Whit Sunday a special charity concert featured Suzette Tarri, Raymond Newall and local musician Leonardi and his Broadcasting Orchestra.

The Odeon did not sustain major damage during the Second World War but it was very close to the ill-fated Metropole Hotel which was devastated in a 1943 air raid.

However, when the Anglo Swiss Hotel was hit during an air raid it was thought that the Odeon had escaped damage but when the screen curtains were opened it was found that shrapnel had penetrated the rear wall and passed through the screen and came to rest in the stalls.

Foyer and cash desk at the Odeon, Lansdowne, late 1940's

In 1946 when the British musical LONDON TOWN was screened, Kay Kendall who starred in the film, made several stage appearances. Former projectionist at the Odeon, Terry Davies (1945-1952) recalls many live star appearances and on the technical side he remembers the installation of B.T.H..SUPA projection equipment, which was the first installation of its kind in the United Kingdom.

Auditorium of the Odeon, Lansdowne, 1950

In 1958 when SOUTH PACIFIC was screened for a season an electronic organ was installed to enhance the presentation. Ronald Brickell who was resident organist at the Gaumont at this time, had a very busy summer season that year playing daily in both cinemas.

The Odeon holds the record for the longest film run in Bournemouth which was achieved in 1965/1966 when THE SOUND OF MUSIC ran for 80 weeks.

Situated as it was away from the main holiday centre of the town possibly contributed to the Odeon being the chosen cinema of the larger venues in Bournemouth for closure. The fact that it was the newest of the three large cinemas in town and very comfortable, spacious and well kept did not appear to be enough to save this attractive theatre after only 37 years of providing film entertainment. In 1973 the policy of two different programmes each day was adopted for several months but even this could not prevent the inevitable and on 16 January 1974 the doors finally closed. The last programme was BIG ZAPPER and THE CONSPIRACY.

The building was then adapted for bingo by the Rank Organisation and continues to be used for this purpose, although not now as part of the Rank Organisation.

The Odeon name still exists in Westover Road where the former Regent/Gaumont became Bournemouth's Odeon providing entertainment on six screens.

Described as Bournemouth's Bijou Cinema De Luxe the 125 seat Premier New Theatre came on the scene in 1936. Situated in Albert Road the Premier was owned and managed by Mr Reginald Ernest Bath, Managing Director of R.E. Bath Travel Services Ltd. The premises were part of the building occupied by the Bournemouth Daily Echo in earlier years.

Due to its popularity the Premier was enlarged and redesigned the following year and seating accommodation was increased to 312.

The original entrance was on the corner of Albert Road and Adelaide Lane but when alterations were carried out the entrance was moved along Albert Road and the projection room was relocated above the main entrance. Architect in charge of the alterations was Mr E. de Wilde Holding, whose offices were in Westover Road.

Initially the programme consisted of two newsreels, a travelogue, interest or comedy short and a cartoon.

Mr Harry Hanby who was associated with the Premier for many years as Manager came to Bournemouth in 1943 from the Rialto, Leeds.

In 1965 the cinema ceased to be known as the Premier News Theatre and became the Premier, when a policy of showing normal feature films was adopted and seating capacity was reduced to 240.

This situation continued another eight years until closure in 1973 when Mr Hanby told the Evening Echo "The days of the second run cinemas are rapidly coming to an end. It's no good waiting until you are losing money and struggling".

Final programme at Bournemouth's Bijou De Luxe Cinema was on 19 September 1973 when Gene Hackman starred in THE FRENCH CONNECTION.

Front entrance, Premier Cinema, Albert Road, Bournemouth 1970

Also in Albert Road the New Royal Threatre (formerly the Theatre Royal) was presenting regular film programmes in the 1960's. They specialised in double feature programmes of classic films of yester-year. Typical offerings in May 1963 were SINGING IN THE RAIN coupled with THE GREAT CARUSO and NORTH BY NORTHWEST with the MARX BROTHERS GO WEST.

In July 1971 the upper floor of the theatre became Bournemouth's first cinema club. The Tatler seated 350 and programmes mainly consisted of uncensored material and films not usually available in commercial cinemas. The Tatler was well equipped and decorated with new seating and furnishings, Kalee '20' projectors were imported from a cinema at Frome, Somerset.

Films have been shown at various other venues in central Bournemouth over the years. Shortly after opening in 1929 the Pavilion Theatre was presenting silent films and on occasions the musical accompaniment was provided by the Bournemouth Municipal Orchestra conducted by Sir Dan Godfrey.

The Winter Gardens Theatre has also presented feature film shows at various times, mainly on a seasonal basis.

The Palace Court Theatre in Hinton Road which opened in 1931 was primarily used for stage presentations but had facilities for screening films which continued when it became the Playhouse Theatre in more recent years.

When the Playhouse was in use as a theatre in the 1970's and 1980's the lower floor became the Galaxy Cinema for some years and although open throughout the year in the summer months often presented extended runs of popular films to attract the holiday trade.

Architect, Mr C H Fowler, who was involved with the design of several local cinemas that have already been mentioned, recalls that in 1936 he designed a 2000 seat cinema to be built on a site at the back of the old bus station in The Square. At about the same time plans were also made for a 1000 seater near Five Ways in Charminster and a possible News Theatre at the Lansdowne adjacent to Yauners the tobacconists. None of these proposals were proceeded with but it may be of interest to learn of three cinemas that Bournemouth nearly acquired in the 1930s.

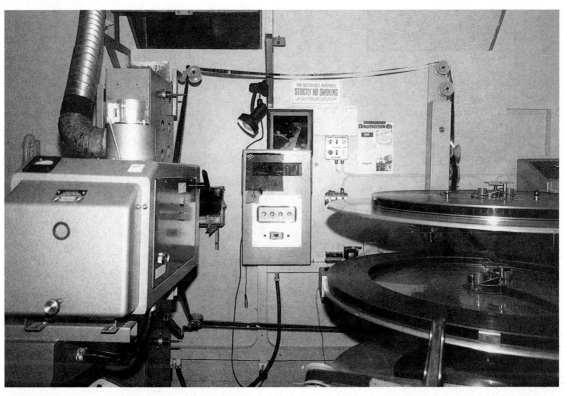

Projection room, Galaxy Cinema, Hinton Road, Bournemouth 1986

Projection room, Play House, Hinton Road, Bournemouth 1986

Winton and Moordown

The Winton Hall at 303 Wimborne Road was designed by local architect, Mr Frederick Fogarty, and built in 1908 for use as an assembly hall for various local activities. It is possible that in the first few years of its existence bioscope shows were occasionally given here but it was not until December 1911 when the Bournemouth Visitors' Directory announced that the newest novelty pictures would be shown continuously each day from 6 p.m. until 10 p.m. with matinees on Saturdays and Wednesdays, that the Winton area really had its own Picture Palace. Highest seat price was one shilling (5p) for the grand circle.

The following year the Winton Hall changed its name to Winton Electric Picture House and continued as such until the lease was acquired by the late Alderman Harry Mears OBE in 1929 when the cinema became the Plaza. Records show that in late 1928 for a short time before the name Plaza was announced the cinema advertised as the New and Popular Palace - Winton's Superior Cinema.

Mr Mears had been involved in the cinema business from the early years of the century. He came to Bournemouth from London primarily for health reasons but soon became involved with cinemas in the town, an association which lasted nearly fifty years and included many cinemas in Bournemouth and other towns in Hampshire and Dorset. In the 1930's he had an interest in the Empire, Wareham and the Palace at Bridport. Quite apart from his cinema activities which included Presidency of the Cinematograph Exhibition's Association in 1951/1952, Mr Mears was three times Mayor of Bournemouth and a Freeman of the Borough.

Plaza, Winton, Bournemouth 1936

Prior to the opening of the Plaza, Winton extensive renovations were carried out by a London company under the supervision of Mr Friese-Green, son of one of the pioneers of the film industry. Electricity was generated by a gas engine in the basement which was completely overhauled and two new Erniman projectors were installed.

When the Plaza re-opened it still retained its distinctive style which featured fancy plasterwork and statues on pillars within the auditorium and externally the unusual tower and pillared cupola which had been likened to a pagoda or Bavarian hunting lodge.

It was claimed that the Plaza was the first Bournemouth cinema to show talking pictures but the author has not been able to definitely confirm this.

Councillor Harry Mears with Charles Chaplin, Bournemouth 1951

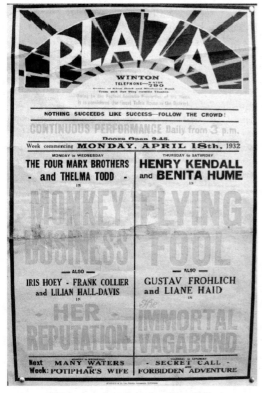

1932, poster found during demolition

Continental Cinema, Winton. Special Laurel and Hardy
convention in November 1987

In 1953 the 420 seat cinema closed for two weeks for redecoration and re-opened as the Continental on 6 April 1953 with the feature film RASHOMON.

Mr Jack Southern who in previous years had managed the Grand at Westbourne, acquired the lease from Mr Mears in 1978 and continued the general policy of second runs and special seasons of classic feature films, Disney productions and other more sexually explicit programmes.

After considerable efforts Mr Southern was unsuccessful in renewing the lease in 1989 and after nearly 77 years the doors closed at Winton's original cinema which was said to be the oldest independently owned cinema in the country.

The last presentation at the Continental was on 8 June 1989 when a somewhat inappropriately name film entitled HIGH HOPES was the main feature.

Within weeks of closure the building was demolished and the site cleared. After approximately six years the site remains empty and derelict.

The Victoria Cinema which was part of the Victoria Parade in Wimborne Road served Winton and Moordown from July 1928 when one of the first films was THE SMALL BACHELOR starring Barbara Kent.

Ten years later when the Victoria was extensively renovated ownership passed to Portsmouth Town Cinemas who were also proprietors of the nearby Moderne Cinema which opened in 1935. The Victoria was renamed the Ritz and then seated approximately 700.

The cinema was redecorated throughout and new projection equipment installed.

Talent competitions were always popular at the Ritz and some local residents who were children in the 1930's and 1940's can recall the excitement of appearing on stage at the Ritz in the weekly contests, which by all accounts were great fun although the prizes were quite modest, usually tickets for future programmes at the Ritz or Moderne.

In 1950 the Ritz was closed for repairs and modernisation. The grand reopening took place in October 1950 when TONY DRAWS A HORSE was screened. Derek Bond who starred in this film made a live appearance on stage to celebrate the reopening. The Ritz continued in operation until April 1959 when the programme for the last week was a sequence of classic films of earlier years.

The entrance to the Ritz was in the centre of the shopping parade and is now barely distinguishable but externally the auditorium is intact although its present use as a motor spares depot has meant many internal alterations.

Messrs Bolton and Mackeen who were in the long distance road transport business, were responsible for the construction of the Moderne Cinema at the junction of Brassey and Wimborne

Roads, which was the site of their original garage.

Architect for the Moderne was Mr E de Wilde Holding L.R.I.B.A. who was involved with several cinema designs in this part of Southern England during the 1930's.

Modernistic plasterwork and decorations were a feature of the design and provision was made for a theatre organ which in fact was never installed.

Opening day at the Moderne was 11 October 1935 when the double feature programme was MUSIC IN THE AIR starring John Boles and BARNACLE BILL starring Denis O'Neil who was in attendance on stage throughout the opening week.

An attractive cafe and ice cream lounge was situated adjacent to the balcony foyer. Seating 1500 the Moderne brought Winton and Moordown the latest cinema design and film presentation in an area where there had been considerable population growth in the period since the First World War. The picture throw from the projector to screen was 186 feet which was unusually long for a cinema of this size.

Within two years of opening the ownership of the Moderne passed to Portsmouth Town Cinemas. After approximately 28 years of films the Moderne went over to Bingo in 1963.

The final film was shown on 25 May 1963 when Peter Sellers starred in WRONG ARM OF THE LAW. After suitable alterations bingo commenced the following month and still continues in the building which remains largely unaltered.

Front cover of souvenir programme for the opening of the Moderne Cinema, Winton 11 October 1935

Moderne Cinema, Winton 1989

Boscombe and Pokesdown

In the Boscombe and Pokesdown area screen entertainment was available at the Grand Theatre (later the Hippodrome) from as early as February 1897. The films were shown as an addition to the usual theatrical programme and were presented by Birt Acre's Royal CINEMATOGRAPHE. Edison's Animated Pictures were also regularly featured at the Grand around the turn of the century.

It is interesting to note that some 50 years later two of the most popular cinema stars of all time appeared live on stage at the Hippodrome when Laurel and Hardy were on tour in the United Kingdom in August 1947. They appeared twice nightly for one week and were enthusiastically received by capacity audiences.

In 1950 Old Mother Riley (Arthur Lucan) was appearing in pantomime at the Hippodrome and at least two local cinemas cashed in on the publicity and screened Old Mother Riley films. At the Ritz, Winton, OLD MOTHER RILEY, HEADMISTRESS was on the programme and closer to the Hippodrome the Savoy was showing OLD MOTHER RILEY'S NEW ADVENTURE.

Just prior to the First World War films were regularly shown at The Clarence in the former Pokesdown Art and Technical School and at about the same time the Boscombe Cinema came into existence at 12 Palmerston Road in a building converted for the purpose. It appears that in the early years of the Boscombe Cinema seating was fairly basic, wooden seats and benches were the order of the day, but during the 1920's things were made more comfortable and at this time seating was for approximately 350 on one floor.

In 1929 Mr Harry Mears acquired the Picture House, as it was then known, and employed Mrs Doris Hartless as pianist. Sound had not yet arrived at the Picture House. Mrs Hartless was to remain with Mr Mears for the next fifty years, serving in several cinemas in various capacities.

In 1930 the Picture House became the Scala and within three years was renamed the New Scala, but in the late 1930's ceased to be a cinema and eventually became the Boscombe Palais until the mid 1950's when it was used as garage premises.

Boscombe New Picture House which was situated almost opposite the Hippodrome Theatre in Christchurch Road, opened in 1915 and boasted a "delightful orchestra and tea lounge and the finest picture house outside London". Musically the New Picture House had another claim to fame as pianist Ernest Lush who became an international musician in later years once regularly played the accompaniment to silent films in this cinema.

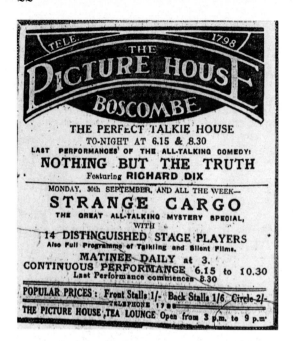

The auditorium was well appointed throughout with velvet curtains and quality seating in stalls and circle, and two special boxes.

In 1930 the building was renovated and redecorated and reopened as the Savoy Cinema. On August 18 1930 fire broke out in the projection room whilst a Mickey Mouse cartoon was being shown and within minutes the building was engulfed, but fortunately with no loss of life or injury to patrons and staff.

Approximately four months later the Savoy reopened on Boxing Day 1930 after reconstruction. Builders were Messrs Jenkins & Sons of Bournemouth and the building was completely refurbished by Messrs Maple & Co. Seating was for 750 and proprietors were M & O Theatres Ltd based in London, who were also involved with the Astoria at Pokesdown in later years. The first film presented in the new Savoy was WELCOME DANGER starring Harold Lloyd.

The Savoy continued to show films for another 28 years until the autumn of 1958 when the final programme included Clayton Moore as THE LONE RANGER on 27 September 1958. The cinema was eventually demolished and the site is now occupied by shops and offices.

In 1931 another cinema came on the scene in Christchurch Road, Boscombe when the Carlton Super Cinema opened its doors for the first time. Seating 1600 in stalls and circle the Carlton was decorated throughout in an oriental style which was unusual and very attractive. The light fittings were a particular feature and gave an effect of opulence and warmth, both in the auditorium and entrance foyer.

The opening film at the Carlton on 27 July 1931 was ONCE A SINNER starring Dorothy Mackail.

Mr William Thornton was the first manager at the Carlton. In earlier years he had been assistant manager at the original Westover Cinema.

Mr Thornton was responsible for a regular entry in the annual Boscombe Carnival with a topical float, which of course included maximum publicity for the current film presentation at the Carlton.

Associated British Cinemas (ABC) ran the Carlton from the beginning but the cinema was not originally built for this Company. For many years the Carlton ran the same programme as the ABC Grand at Westbourne but when the Grand passed from ABC's ownership in 1957 the Carlton often ran the same programme as the larger ABC Westover in Westover Road.

The Carlton closed for modernisation in April 1971 and reopened 29 April with the feature UP POMPEII starring Frankie Howard. The stalls seating was upgraded at this time to Pullman type seats, but this did not forestall the onward march of bingo which took over in 1974 when films ceased at the ABC Boscombe as it was then known. The final film was THE DOVE which was screened on 10 July 1974.

Bingo continued for some years and for a period it became club premises but finally closed in 1988.

The building is reasonably intact but now derelict and unused.

The Astoria in Christchurch Road at Pokesdown was independently owned and operated. Originally seating 1500 the Astoria opened on 24 October 1932 with Wallace Beery in HELL DIVERS and ONE GOOD TURN starring Laurel and Hardy.

The auditorium was rather plain and bare in comparison to many cinemas of this period but

Grand Opening Attractions !

Commencing To-day (Monday) at 2.15, for Six Days Only

Wallace Beery and Clark Gable
— in —

HELL DIVERS

The Greatest Aerial Drama Ever Made ! ! !

ALSO

LAUREL and HARDY
— in —

ONE GOOD TURN

In Their Latest Side-Splitting Comedy ! ! !

UNIVERSAL SOUND NEWS

Prices : 7d. 9d. 1/- 1/3 1/6 and 2/- (including Tax)

there was a Compton theatre organ which was used quite extensively in the 1930's and 1940's by guest organists, who usually gave three organ interludes each day. The side elevation of the building in Queensland Road is quite unusual in respect of the large number of small windows. Most cinema auditoria are rather plain externally but this is certainly not so in this instance.

The Astoria continued to operate as a cinema until 1964 when regular film presentation ceased and bingo was introduced.

Towards the end of its life as a cinema the Astoria became part of Harry Mears group of cinemas.

The final film programme was on 23 May 1964 when the double feature screened was Robert Taylor in VALLEY OF KINGS and PRIVATE PROGRESS starring Richard Attenborough.

The building still remains very much as it was originally and is still used as a venue for bingo.

Astoria Cinema, Pokesdown 1993

Southbourne

In October 1919 cinema entertainment came to Southbourne. Local entrepreneur Mr J Newbury was the proprietor and manager of the Palladium, Fisherman's Walk, which opened on 6 October 1919 screening THE ORDEAL OF ROSETTA and a comedy OFFICER JERRY.

The advertising for Southbourne's new cinema made it clear that the orchestra was absolutely first class and that the Palladium was "The finest ventilated hall in the provinces". Popular prices were the order of the day with two changes of programme weekly. Seating approximately 550 the cinema was situated conveniently in the main commercial area at Southbourne.

Ownership changed several times over the years and in the 1930's the Palladium became part of the Portsmouth Town Cinema group, and even-tually one of Harry Mear's cinemas. In 1948 the Palladium closed for renovations and reopened on 1 July 1948 renamed the Embassy. First programme under the new name was DESERT FURY starring John Hodiak. Six years later after further alterations and renovation the management announced a radical new policy featuring "The pick of the world's films past and present".

The cinema was renamed the Classic at this time and the grand reopening was on Easter Monday 1954 when the 1933 Academy Award performance by Charles Laughton in THE PRIVATE LIFE OF HENRY VIII was screened at "Southbourne's Bijou Cinema", as it was sometimes known.

The Classic lasted another six years still in the ownership of Mr Mears but sadly went the way of so many of the smaller cinemas and the last film TOWN ON TRIAL was presented on Saturday, 30 September 1960. The building was then converted for use as a supermarket.

Palladium, West Southbourne on opening day 6th October 1919

Springbourne

Prior to the opening of the Coronation Picture Palace in Holdenhurst Road the Springbourne area enjoyed occasional film shows at the Drill Hall. One of the earliest of such shows was in 1904 when a Grand Trades Exhibition presented free cinematograph entertainment.

The Coronation Picture Palace opened on 24 June 1911 and included in the first programme was a film of the recent Coronation of King George V and Queen Mary.

The Proprietors of the Coronation in the early days were a Mr Birchmore and a Mr Linden who were involved with the running of concert parties and other such shows on Bournemouth sea front. In the early days of the cinema a wide variety of entertainment was provided, both live shows and films of all types. There was a resident orchestra in the "silent" days and the theatre was equipped with a pipe organ.

The owner of the Coronation during the 1920's and 1930's was Mr J Clafton and late in 1936 there was a change of name when it became the Roxy. Four years later in 1940 Mr Harry Mears became lessee of the Roxy until the Luftwaffe came on the scene in 1943/1944.

When West's Cinema in Central Bournemouth was destroyed by enemy action in May 1943, the proprietors Mr & Mrs R A Pope took over the lease of the Roxy from Mr Mears and after renovations reopened the cinema on 20 January 1944, now renamed West's Pictures.

Another incendiary bomb raid in April 1944 destroyed the newly created West's Pictures and it remained in a ruined state for approximately six years awaiting a post war building licence for this type of construction.

On 9 March 1950 the Roxy reappeared on the entertainment map in Springbourne.

Architects, W J Dacombe & Son of Boscombe and D F Hillier, Parkstone builders were responsible for the reconstruction of the Roxy.

Mr & Mrs Pope continued to be the joint lessees of the new 600 seat Roxy and the opening feature film on 9 March 1950 was BLUE SKIES starring Bing Crosby and Fred Astaire.

The Roxy continued as a cinema until 1963 when it became the Roxy Bingo on 28 August. The last film programme was on the previous Sunday, 25 August when BLIND DATE starring Stanley Baker was screened.

The Roxy Bingo Club closed in January 1994 and the premises are currently used as a photographic workshop and laboratory, so after eighty-four years the site continues to have a connection with films, but very different from those early silent moving pictures way back in 1911.

Westbourne

Just prior to Christmas in 1922 Westbourne welcomed its own cinema/theatre when the Grand opened in Poole Road.

The first attraction was a stage production of ANTONY AND CLEOPATRA. On Boxing Day the main film was A PRINCE OF LOVERS and the supporting programme included a Harold Lloyd comedy and an edition of the GAUMONT GRAPHIC.

The Grand Super Cinema/Theatre was well appointed and a worthy addition to Bournemouth's cinemas. Seating 1000 the Grand incorporated several unusual features including a sliding section in the roof which could be opened on warm summer evenings. Some local people can recall that when the roof was open the noisy clatter of the trams passing along Poole Road could be more than a little distracting. There was also a lift to the balcony and cafe. High on the roof overlooking Poole Road there was a revolving globe which was illuminated at night. Carter's Architectural Tiles were used on the frontage of the building and in the auditorium the orchestra pit screen was also faced with tiles from Carter's pottery at Poole.

In the 1920's the Grand claimed to have Bournemouth's finest Picture Orchestra under the direction of Capt. W A Featherstone who was also musical director of Bournemouth Wireless Orchestra at 6BM the local BBC station.

In 1930 just after the "talkies" arrived the Grand's chief projectionist, J Trevisone, had an article published in the Bournemouth and Southampton Graphic which described in some detail the process of cinema film projection from the point of view of a film that was being shown to an audience.

In the early years of the Grand's existence many patrons were drawn from the Branksome and Parkstone areas as the Victory Palace at Upper Parkstone was modest in size and accommodation and lacked some of the refinements of a modern purpose built cinema. This situation changed when the Regal replaced the Victory Palace at Parkstone in 1935.

Originally independently owned the Grand was taken over in the early 1930's by Savoy Cinemas and in 1935 became part of the ABC circuit, which gave this Company three cinemas in Bournemouth. The Carlton at Boscombe and the Grand often ran the same programme during the 1950's and 60's.

In December 1953 ABC disposed of the Grand to Northern based Snape Entertainments and regular films continued until 1973 when on 8 October the last full time programme was presented. THEY LOVE SEX was on the screen that last evening after 51 years of regular films at this cinema.

The next four years the pattern at the Grand was a mixture of films and bingo until 1977 when the last film at Westbourne's one and only cinema was IN LOVE WITH SEX, which sounds rather similar to the programme some four years previously.

Since 1977 the Grand has continued to offer bingo and the building is very little changed from its original form.

Grand Cinema, Westbourne 1922

BRIDPORT

The Bridport News in January 1912 reported that as soon as alterations were completed and an electrical power plant was installed the Old Artillery Hall in Barrack Street would open as the Bridport Electric Palace Cinema. The opening programme was on 26 February 1912 and included in the programme were the films MAIDEN OF THE PIE FACED INDIANS, NIAGARA FALLS and SIEGE OF CALAIS. Proprietor of the cinema was Mr C Sheppard whose son Sydney was subsequently involved with cinema management in Bridport for many years. In the 1920's there occurred an accident at the Electric Palace involving nitrate film stored near the gas engine and the operator Billy Ryan had a lucky escape when fire broke out which could be very serious with this type of film stock.

In 1925 the new Electric Palace opened on a site previously occupied by a coal yard. Local brewery owner J C Palmer had the idea of a new theatre for Bridport but it was realised that the area could not support solely theatrical shows and Sydney Sheppard was persuaded to close the old Bridport Electric Palace in Barrack Street. The new theatre was fully equipped for entertainment and stage productions, including a unit which was known as The Phantom Orchestra to accompany the silent films of the period. The unit consisted of two piano roll players and sound effects. The last film at the Old Palace on 29 May 1926 was SIEGE starring Virginia Vallis and a cartoon featuring Felix the Cat.

Thus it was that the new Electric Palace in South Street with seating for 543 on two floors was opened on Monday, 14 June 1926 by Bridport's Mayor, Mr F Weeks. Mr J C Palmer, Chairman of the Directors, entertained all concerned with the new cinema enterprise to dinner at the Greyhound Hotel the same evening.

Due to the fact that mains electricity was not available in Bridport until 1930 the new theatre was equipped with its own power plant powered by Town gas engines which gave many years of service, even after mains electricity became available. The architects were Messrs Frederick Cooper and Sons of Bridport and the main building contractors were Jesty and Baker of Weymouth. Projection and stage equipment was supplied by Walturdaw Ltd.

One slightly unusual feature in the auditorium was the provision of two boxes each seating five persons at the rear of the circle. The first programme at the New Electric Palace starred Gloria Swanson in MADAME SANS GENE.

Advertising for the new cinema often referred to the "Cosiest Little Theatre in the County" and in the 1920's and 30's the local press gave details of special evening bus services tailored to programmes at the Electric Palace. These services were arranged by several local companies and brought patrons from Beaminster, Burton Bradstock, Charmouth and many other villages around Bridport. During the mid 1930's local artist George Biles who painted inn signs and similar items, added extensive mural decorations at the Palace which brightened up the rather plain interior. Although the auditorium murals were painted over in the 1950's the foyer and stairway still retain the murals which make an attractive and unusual feature.

The mobile Hayes Theatre which toured the area for many years with portable equipment finally came to rest at Bridport in 1934. Mr Church and Mr Stevenson acquired some of the materials to fit out the old Bridport Palace in Barrack Street which was opened as the Lyric Cinema on 17 December 1934 with the double feature FOOTLIGHT PARADE starring James Cagney and Alice Faye in GEORGE WHITE SCANDALS. The following year 1935 saw an unusual show at the Palace in South Street "Romance of the Music Hall" was presented in August for three days starring live on stage Billy Cotton and his Band and Nellie Wallace. Films were the usual presentations at this time with the odd week or two each year when local operatic and musical societies presented live entertainment, including an annual pantomime.

Mr Frank Crescioli, who was chief projectionist at the Palace in the early 1940's, recalls that both cinemas were very well patronised during the war years and Sunday programmes were shared by the Lyric and the Palace which meant reels of film being smartly on the move at all times between the two cinemas on Sunday evenings.

The Dorchester Cinema Company, proprietors of the Plaza, Dorchester, took over the Palace and Lyric in 1940. The Lyric which seated approximately 200 continued to function until 1962 when, due to falling attendances, the management told the Bridport News that "We consider that one cinema in the town is sufficient". Final film at the Lyric on 1 September 1962 was THE SECRET PARTNER starring Stewart Grainger.

The Palace in later years had several different proprietors including some years as part of the Myles Byrne group of country town cinemas.

Reeltime Entertainment based in Kent, who are proprietors of the Carlton, Westgate on Sea and the Torbay Picture House, acquired the Palace in 1992. Improvements and modernisa

Bridport Electric Palace in the 1920's later to become the Lyric

Projector and original "Sound on Disc" equipment, Palace Cinema, Bridport 1920's

tions have been made and more are planned for the future.

Jim Carter who took over the day to day running of the Palace in 1994, including the projec-tion room, found much to his surprise that the Cinemeccania 18 projector at the Palace is the machine that he installed originally at the Savoy, Andover in 1971.

Circle foyer showing murals in the Palace, Bridport 1994

Cinemeccania 18 projector in the Palace, Bridport 1994

CHRISTCHURCH

Local entrepreneur Mr Frederick Pope was responsible for the first permanent cinema at Christchurch in 1914. Prior to this date in common with many other small towns Christchurch had to await the visits of travelling showmen with their fairground bioscope shows. Alternatively residents of the town had to visit Bournemouth to see the latest offerings on the silver screens of West's Pictures, the Coronation Cinema in Holdenhurst Road, or possibly the Electric Cinema in central Bournemouth, all of whom had been in business for some years prior to 1914.

The Royal Cinema Theatre at 65 Bargates opened on 9 July 1914. The Mayor, R Druitt Esq. officiated at this ceremony and it appears that the first programme was a matinee featuring a musical recital by a pianist and a vocalist. The first film programme at the 400 seat Royal included LOVE AND GASOLINE which was billed as a "Screaming Keystone Comedy".

Advertising in 1915 for the Royal announced that soldiers in uniform would be admitted at half price and reassuringly that the auditorium was disinfected daily with Jeyes Fluid.

Just prior to Christmas in 1919 the Royal became the New Gaiety Picture House and was then described as a very warm and cosy cinema. In the summer of 1920 several live stage productions were presented and in May MY OLD DUTCH was staged at the Gaiety starring Albert Chevalier in the leading role.

In the late summer of 1921 the Gaiety became the Pavilion Electric Theatre and subsequently the Pavilion Cinema and Dance Hall.

Formerly Royal Cinema Theatre, Bargates,
Christchurch 1994

During the 1920's the Pavilion offered films of local events in some programmes. In 1928 when the main feature film was THE FLIGHT COMMANDER starring Sir Alan Cobham included in the programme were exclusive pictures of Christchurch Hospital Carnival. Other local events were screened at the Pavilion, often on the same days as they occurred.

Sid Clark who became circuit engineer with Mr Geoffrey Bravery at Poole in later years started his career in the projection room of the Pavilion in the "silent" days.

In 1931 the Regent Super Cinema opened in the High Street. Mr F J Rowley who had been responsible for the building of the Carlton at Boscombe and the Victoria at Winton, built the £25,000 Regent with the intention that it would be as good or better than cinemas in adjoining towns, particularly bearing in mind the competition from Bournemouth's luxury cinemas.

The 700 seat Regent opened on Boxing Day 1931 with the film TAMING OF THE SHREW starring Mary Pickford and Douglas Fairbanks.

Early in 1933 the Pavilion closed for redecorations and alterations and the Christchurch Times reported that the newly painted murals in the auditorium depicting country scenes would delight future audiences. The Pavilion reopened on 14 February 1933 with THE BIG BROADCAST starring a host of musical stars including Bing Crosby.

Ten months later in December 1933 Mr W A Wimbleton who held the controlling interest in the Pavilion formed a small local syndicate and acquired the Regent.

Despite the recent expenditure on the Pavilion the Bargates cinema was closed and the final film on 10 December 1933 was BIG CAGE supported by the 10th episode of the serial THE JUNGLE MYSTERY.

The Pavilion cinema building has been used for various purposes over the years and currently it houses the Christchurch Branch of the Royal British Legion.

Portsmouth Town Cinemas were proprietors of the Regent from the mid 1930's but at the time of closure as a cinema in July 1973 it was in the ownership of the ABC circuit.

On 18 July the Regent screened THE THIEF WHO CAME TO DINNER starring Ryan O'Neal and John Wayne in THE TRAIN ROBBERS and then the Mecca Organization took over and bingo came to the Regent until closure in February 1982.

Christchurch Borough Council bought the cinema and a team of local enthusiasts with expert assistance transformed the building into a multi-purpose entertainment centre which reopened in June 1983.

Live stage shows, exhibitions and a regular showing of current film releases has really given the Regent a new lease of life.

In recent years seating has been improved and new projection equipment and sound system has been installed. Every effort has been made to maintain the 1930's style of the Regent which certainly continues to be a focal point for entertainment in the town.

Regent Cinema, Christchurch 1993

DORCHESTER

The earliest moving picture entertainment in Dorchester was not a projected picture show but an unusual sequence of painted pictures with commentary, sound effects and special lighting. The scenes were on large canvas rolls which moved across the stage between two sets of rollers and portrayed subjects such as the Boer

Advertisement for Poole's "Myriorama" Moving Picture Shows, early 1900's

War, The Royal Naval Review at Spithead or other important Royal occasions.

These "Myriorama" shows toured Great Britain and Ireland from the middle of the last century. The Poole family, who were based in Kent presented their "Myriorama" at the Corn Exchange, Dorchester in March and October 1903. Local bill poster George Lawton of Durngate Street distributed posters for these shows around the Dorchester area. Records show that he continued to handle posters for theatrical and film shows in the town for many years.

One of the earliest film shows at the Corn Exchange was in November 1909 when a Dr Seaton presented a programme which was advertised as "All the latest animated pictures". The following month in December Albany Ward was presenting Perfect Picture Entertainment at the Corn Exchange - direct from the Jubilee Hall, Weymouth. Included in this programme was a film epic entitled THE AIRSHIP DESTROYER.

Dorchester Electric Picturedrome in Durngate Street was presenting twice nightly film shows and Saturday matinees in 1911. Interestingly the Kelly's county directory for 1911 gives only three cinemas in the whole county of Dorset - namely, the Amity Picture Palace and Electric Theatre at Poole and Dorchester Electric Picturedrome. Just prior to the First World War the "Electric" was dropped and it became the Dorchester Picturedrome.

Other locations in the town where film entertainment was provided from time to time included the former Georgian theatre at the top of Trinity Street and on the first floor of the property on the corner of Trinity Street and High West Street, which is now in use as a cafe.

In 1920 the Picturedrome became the Palace Theatre under the ownership of Albany Ward who had been trying for some years to acquire premises in the town to provide entertainment similar to that available in his venues at Weymouth.

Extensive rebuilding and alterations were undertaken at the old Picturedrome under the direction of local architect, Mr F T Maltby. Main building work was carried out by Messers Jesty and Baker of Weymouth.

The opening ceremony of the new Palace Theatre was on Tuesday 2 November 1920 when Mr Van den Bergh, General Manager of the Award Circuit (Albany Ward) welcomed invited guests including the Mayor and Mayoress, Mr and Mrs A Tilley, Mrs Thomas Hardy and many members of the Town Council.

The Palace accommodated 400 in stalls and circle and was equipped with every modern facility, and the latest type of projection equipment. The Dorset County Chronicle reported "So far as the bioscope side is concerned, the operating chamber is equipped with duplicate machines as the result of which there will be no irksome waits between the pictures". The first film presentation was POSSESSION starring Harry Edwards, also in the programme was the first episode of a serial THE SILENT MYSTERY and an edition of PATHE GAZETTE.

Former Dorchester resident, Mr Harry Johnston, recalls his involvement with the Palace during the 1920's. As a boy he assisted with the distribution of Palace play bills and posters and in 1925 became the "Chocolate Boy" in the cinema to augment his wages as an apprentice printer. Through his acquaintance with one of the projectionists he came to assist with sound effects when the film SEA HAWK (silent version) was shown in August 1925. Due to his enthusiasm he added to the existing equipment and succeeded in getting various sound effects mixed up which met with strong words from the management.

Mr Johnston also remembers regular talent competitions between the films at the Palace and in particular local young star Bert Coleman's impression of the old music hall song "Burlington Bertie".

Former Palace Theatre, Dorchester, originally Electric Picturedrome

In the mid 1920's ownership passed to Provincial Cinematograph Theatres and in the late 1930's the Gaumont British Corporation took control. One slightly unusual feature of the Palace was that on the front of the building facing Durngate Street there was a short iron catwalk along which the projectionist walked from the projection room to the rewind room between reels.

The Palace continued to bring the latest films to Dorchester until 1957 when the Rank Organization decided that closure was inevitable due mainly to falling attendances and the crippling entertainment tax which was badly affecting so many cinemas at this time.

Last programme at the Palace was on 6 May 1957 when Van Johnson starred in the film KELLY AND ME. Several members of the staff were long serving and much regretted the closure and commented that Rebecca the Ghost who was said to have been at the Palace for many years, would miss them and the nightly audiences of film-goers. Even on the day of closure the Palace Cinema Children's Club was well supported with over 300 children for the Saturday morning show which was always popular with Dorchester's youngsters.

The Plaza Cinema in Trinity Street was opened by the Dorchester Cinema Company on 10 July 1933. Major W P Colfox, M.P. for West Dorset performed the opening ceremony of the town's new entertainment venue. The opening programme was KING KONG and this was said to be the first showing of this film outside London, and direct from the London Coliseum. Seating was for 986 and the Plaza was advertised as being one of the finest theatres in the provinces. Adjoining the balcony was a cafe providing patrons with refreshments in comfortable surroundings.

During the Second World War the Plaza was much used by official organizations for instructional and fund raising events. For example on 3rd November 1941 there was a Ministry of Information talk by Mr Bernard Newman - World's Greatest Espionage authority on "V" or "Hitler over Europe" - illustrated by lantern slides. Two days after D-Day in 1944 a special War Savings Campaign concert was given at the Plaza featuring Isobel Baillie, Heddle Nash and Harry Hemsley. The cinema was also much used by the American Army for lectures and special film shows, particularly in the period just prior to D-Day.

In 1978 the cinema was considerably altered internally when in the ownership of Zetters. Provision was made in the stalls area for Bingo and two auditoria seating 200 and 100 approximately were created on the first floor. Subsequently the Plaza became part of the Myles Byrne cinema group who had several other cinemas in Dorset during the 1960/1980 period.

In 1991 the Kent based company Reeltime Entertainment took over the Plaza and many improvements have been made. Seating has been refurbished, the foyer has been remodelled and many other renovations are planned. The latest projection equipment has now been installed and the general upgrading of technical facilities is proposed.

When Reeltime took over one of their directors, Barry Kavanagh, stated that "Our aim is to put Dorchester back on the cinema map. It is a great little town and people are beginning to appreciate that the cinema is here to stay".

Plaza Cinema, Dorchester 1993

GILLINGHAM

The market hall that once existed near the railway station was Gillingham's earliest cinema. It was known as Walford's Electric Picture Palace. The proprietor was Mr Charlie Walford who was also involved with mobile cinema shows in villages around the Blackmore Vale, in the early days of film entertainment in this part of Dorset. More about Mr Walford in the section dealing with village film shows.

Mr R W M Robinson in 1911 opened a new picture house in Buckingham Road. This was a new building with the cinema upstairs and the ground floor was a men's club. This cinema was known as the Gillingham Palace. The Palace had its own monthly magazine and in the August 1933 edition it mentioned a film entitled THE KING'S CUP in which Sir Alan Cobham featured. Probably no one at that time realised how much Sir Alan Cobham would be involved in Dorset life in later years with his Flight Refuelling Company at Tarrant Rushton and Wimborne.

Also in the same Palace magazine of 1933 it mentions Three Counties Motors who apparently ran a special coach each evening to "Gillingham Talkies" from Wincanton, Bourton, Zeals and Mere.

In 1933 Mr Robinson had the Regal Cinema built which opened on 10 January 1934 with the film THE LOST CHORD. After the Regal was opened films were no longer shown at the Palace.

The Regal, built by Williams Bros. of Shaftesbury, was designed by architect, Mr E De Wilde Holding who was at this time designing cinemas in Somerset, Devon and Dorset. According to the architect's chief assistant, Mr C H Fowler, there was difficulty regarding the floor covering in the foyer and auditorium as workers from a nearby pig processing plant contaminated the floor with their boots, so an especially resistant material had to be used. By all accounts the Regal was an intimate, luxurious and cosy cinema and seated 300 patrons in comfort.

The Regal passed into the hands of Bassett Cinemas when Mr Robinson retired. This company also owned the Savoy at Shaftesbury and the Plaza at Wincanton.

In 1963 the Regal was finally closed. The last programme was on Sunday, 20 October 1963 with the double feature LEGION OF THE DOOMED and THE RISE AND FALL OF LEGS DIAMOND.

Within weeks of closure the Regal was demolished and shops were built on the site.

The Regal Cinema, Gillingham just after opening in 1934

HAMWORTHY

The building in Blandford Road, Hamworthy, which eventually became the Empire Cinema, was built in the 1920's and in the early 1930's was used for a variety of purposes.

Wrestling, roller skating, variety shows and a period as a Salvation Army Hall all featured in its early history.

In 1935 Mr Bob Coleman set up business as a cinema in the hall and on August Bank Holiday the Mayor of Poole, Councillor W Stickland, officially opened the Empire. The first programme was Shirley Temple in BABY TAKES A BOW. Seating was for approximately 400 on one floor. The usual pattern of programme was one performance nightly and two performances on Saturday and Sunday although variations were made to suit the circumstances, especially during the wartime period.

Mr Owen Taylor, who was projectionist at the Empire from 1938 until 1959, recalls that the original projectors were Kalee 8's which were reliable but rather noisy.

Two incidents in 1942 caused temporary closure. During the showing of UP THE RIVER a fire occurred in the projection room involving two reels of very inflammable nitrate films which caused a fair amount of damage but after a hectic repair operation over about 24 hours they were back in business the following night. The second incident was caused by an unexploded bomb which fell in Mr Coleman's garden next door to the cinema. There was some delay in the bomb being made safe and the Empire was closed completely for a week. The cinema finally closed in 1959 with the showing of TIGER BAY starring Hayley and John Mills although there was some effort made to provide a show once a week with 16mm equipment as late as 1963.

Local people recall seeing FROM RUSSIA WITH LOVE at the Empire but not whilst it was operating as an established cinema.

Formerly the Empire Cinema, Hamworthy

LYME REGIS

Situated on the western edge of the County the seaside resort of Lyme Regis has been offering film entertainment from the time of the First World War. Mr John Raymond originally presented shows in the Assembly Rooms which were located on the site of the present Cobb Gate car park. Mr Raymond's daughter accompanied the silent films on the piano. In the mid-1920's activities moved to the Drill Hall where Mr Bill Emmett was the proprietor. The town directory of 1931 shows that by then Mr Walter Hardy and his son Donald were managing cinema shows at the Drill Hall which was also known as the Marine Cinema in later years. Advertisements at this time listed "cinema performances, plays and comedies during the season" as some of the attractions on offer at this venue.

When the Guildhall Cinema at Axminster opened with all modern facilities Mr Donald Hardy became aware that some of his regular customers were deserting him for the new cinema and all that it had to offer. It was decided to acquire the site of the Bow House Hotel at the junction of Broad Street and Silver Street and build a new cinema.

The architect appointed was Mr W H Watkins FRIBA of Bristol who had also designed the Gaumont Palace at Exeter, the Forum at Bath and more locally the Regal at Seaton.

The stadium style auditorium with 560 seats was elegantly and tastefully decorated in shades of apricot, green and gold and there was the added attraction of a "Holophane" lighting system which gave the projectionist the option to vary the illumination of the auditorium in many sequences of colours.

The Regent opened on 11 October 1937 and the Bridport News reported that the Mayor of Lyme, the Reverend G H Eyre, told the audience "Patrons want comfort and convenience and that has certainly been provided for them here by Mr Hardy". The builder of the Regent was Mr A S Prince who was based in Bournemouth.

The opening programme featured the film THE LIMPING MAN starring Hugh Wakefield.

During the period from the opening of the Regent until the outbreak of the 2nd World War the Marine Cinema (Drill Hall) continued to be used as a cinema but mainly on a seasonal basis. The building was also used as a Service canteen during the war and the American troops arranged films shows, usually on a Sunday evening.

Projectionist Cyril Wellman worked for Donald Hardy at the Marine Theatre and was in the projection room of the Regent on the opening day in 1937. After a really remarkable record of

Corner of the projection room, Regent Cinema,
Lyme Regis 1994

service in one cinema of 57 years he retired in 1994.

Cyril's memories cover many aspects of life at the Regent including the wartime period when a German raider was shot down in the bay. Mr Hardy stopped the show so that the audience could go outside to see the crew being taken into custody after baling out of the stricken aircraft.

In 1944 there were many Service personnel both British and American in the Lyme Regis area and Cyril recalls special morning shows of battle training films arranged by the military authorities. During this period actor James Cagney visited the Regent to entertain the Americans and as there were no proper stage facilities a temporary stage was provided for this show and James Cagney danced and sang "Yankee Doodle Dandy" as he did in the film of the same name which was released in 1942.

Cyril also remembers the making of ALL OVER THE TOWN which was filmed in Lyme in the 1950's. He was called upon to screen the "rushes" at the Regent and in later years when THE

FRENCH LIEUTENANT'S WOMAN was made on location in Lyme the Regent was again used for this purpose.

Ownership of the Regent passed to Charles Scott Cinemas in the late 1970's and is currently owned by Mr Peter Hoare who runs other cinemas in the West Country, including the Radway at nearby Sidmouth.

Manager Alex Orme confirms that the Regent which now seats around 400 is still doing good business, although in some ways it is inclined to be seasonal in pattern.

Every effort is made to give variety in the films presented and sometimes sequences of films are shown throughout the day and special late night shows for certain films. The remarkable JURASSIC PARK did record business for five weeks in 1993 with long queues and packed houses at every performance.

Mr Peter Hoare has considered converting the Regent into two auditoria as structurally this is quite possible, but at the moment the cinema remains virtually as it was built in 1937 and continues to provide entertainment in this part of West Dorset as originally envisaged by Walter and Donald Hardy 59 years ago.

Regent Cinema, Lyme Regis 1994

PARKSTONE

The earliest cinema in Parkstone was in a small hall near the railway bridge in Sandbanks Road which was opened in 1909 by a Mr Holder. Little is known about this "Bioscope Hall" as it was called in its advertising, but it was also known as the Plaza.

Three or four years later the Whitehall Premier Picture Palace at 51 Ashley Road, Parkstone was in business advertising "Superb pictures, perfect orchestra and the world before you".

The Parkstone Empire at 310 Ashley Road is listed in a directory of 1911 as premises where Bioscope films could be enjoyed.

Mr Sidney Rutter of Branksome confirms that his father managed a small cinema at this address in the years prior to the First World War when it was known as the Bijou. Mr Rutter Senior in later years was manager of Poole Electric Theatre for Mr James Bravery.

The Victory Palace cinema located on the corner of Ashley and Jubilee Roads was in action in 1920. First film programme was GRAFTERS and OUR GIRLS. Programmes at the Victory Palace

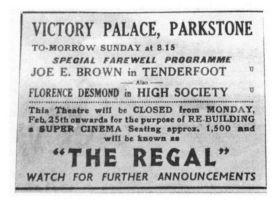

were often a mixture of live variety entertainment and films.

This was another of Mr Bravery's cinemas and continued to provide entertainment into the "talkie" era until it was replaced by the Regal on the same site. The last programme at the Victory Palace was on 24 February 1935 with Joe E Brown starring in TENDERFOOT.

The Regal was built by local builder K Wilson and designed by architect Mr R A Thomas. The opening on 18 September 1935 was attended by civic dignitaries and Mr James Bravery, Managing Director of Regal (Parkstone) Ltd. The Regal was well equipped in every respect with seating for 1200 and a pleasant small cafe on the first floor above the main entrance.

Souvenir opening programme

The first film presentation was PEG OF OLD DRURY starring Anna Neagle and Cedric Hardwicke.

There was a period in 1953 when the spotlight fell upon the Regal. It was decided to equip the cinema for the showing of 3D films. Mr Sid Clark, circuit engineer for Mr Bravery, supervised the technical work involved, which included a new wide screen and on 6 August 1953 Warner Bros.

HOUSE OF WAX opened for an "indefinite season".

It was the only cinema in the area to screen 3D films at this time and coming towards the end of the summer season business was excellent with queues across the car park each day from the time of opening. Prices for admission included viewing spectacles which were returnable after each performance.

The HOUSE OF WAX ran for six weeks followed by SANGAREE also in 3D. The Manager of the Regal at this time was Mr Cyril Parsons who had wide experience in cinema management and had been involved in the 1930s with Oscar Deutsch, the founder of the Odeon cinema circuit.

Known to the Saturday morning childrens' matinee as "Uncle Cyril" Mr Parsons usually appeared on stage each week with competitions and games for the 1200 children, but sometimes they were so exuberant that he had to abandon his "act" and signal the projection room to let them have the next instalment of FLASH GORDON or whatever the current serial that was running.

Whilst carrying out the duties of relief manager at the Regal, Mr Walter West, previously manager of the Amity in Poole, collapsed and died in the foyer of the Regal. At the age of 80 Mr West was truly a veteran in the theatrical and cinema world.

Mr Michael Bravery, son of the managing director, was manager of the Regal at the time of its closure on 12 October 1963.

Final film presentation was COME BLOW YOUR HORN starring Frank Sinatra.

Regal Cinema, Ashley Road, Parkstone 1953

POOLE

The earliest record of public cinematograph entertainment in Poole was on the 13 and 14 November 1896 when Mr John Ablett visited the Amity Hall, Poole with his Theatrograph animated picture show.

East Dorset Herald advertisement for the Amity Hall, Poole November 1896

In the period around the turn of the century Poole residents could also enjoy bioscope film shows when travelling showman Jacob Studt visited Poole Fair each November.

The Amity Hall was built in 1882 on the site of the present Woolworths for the Ancient Order of Oddfellows, but in later years became the Amity Palace of Varieties and as films became popular most programmes were a mixture of live shows and films, until the mid 1920's when films virtually took over.

Pioneer of cinema entertainment in Poole and Bournemouth Mr James Bravery was managing

James Bravery

director of Popular Bioscope Syndicates Ltd. who established Poole Electric Theatre in the High Street in 1911. This cinema occupied former chapel premises - "Near the tram terminus" - according to advertisements at this time. This location would be approximately where Falkland Square is situated today. The first programme at the Poole Electric included the film FLYING A DAY. This cinema continued to operate until the Regent Theatre opened nearby in December 1926. Final film presentation at the Poole Electric was THE FIGHTING EDGE, which was screened on 30 October 1926.

James Bravery's South Coast Theatre Company had been running the Amity for some years and in 1926 former actor and producer, Mr Walter West, was appointed manager of the theatre at a time when there was an orchestra of six musicians to accompany the silent films and the theatrical performers.

Homemade cinema slide announcing collection of eggs
for wounded "Tommies"

In 1931 a new era began at the Amity Cinema. The theatre was fully equipped for sound film presentations and the first "talkie" feature was KING OF THE KHYBER RIFLES starring Victor McLagen, which was presented on 21 July 1931.

> ## AMITY PALACE
> OF VARIETIES, POOLE.   'Phone 103.
> This Theatre is now being equipped with the latest talking equipment and will commence all-talking programmes On MONDAY NEXT, JULY 21st, with VICTOR McLAGLEN in
> ## "King, of the Khyber Rifles"
> The most thrilling Talkie ever heard
> or seen.
> Nightly, Continuous,   Matinee
> 6—10.30.   Saturday at 2.30.

The Amity closed on Sunday, 14 June 1959 with the double feature A LAWLESS STREET and HE LAUGHS LAST.

Walter West was still in the manager's chair on that final evening at the venue of Dorset's first public cinema some sixty three years earlier.

The Regent Theatre was built in 1926 by Mr Bravery's Company which was then known as South Coast Theatres. By any standard it was a quality theatre. Seven dressing rooms, full stage facilities, seating for 1000 and a three manual organ. Opening performance on 4 December 1926, in the presence of the Mayors of Poole and Bournemouth, was Fay Compton's LONDON LOVE.

Until the advent of talkies in the late 1920's programmes were revues, plays and films. When sound came the programmes were almost completely films and in 1931 a new Christie theatre organ was installed which was specially built to the specification of Mr Alex Taylor, a leading organist at this time. The theatre was closed while the Christie organ was installed and re-opened on 4 July 1931 with the film TILLY OF BLOOMSBURY and with Jack Taylor at the organ console.

Staff at the Regent Theatre, Poole in the mid 1930's

Mr Geoffrey Bravery, nephew of James Bravery, joined the Company in 1928 and eventually became managing director of South Coast Theatre and other associated cinema enterprises.

During the Second World War many broadcasts were made from the Regent, primarily for H.M. Forces and Service charities.

The frontage of the Regent was of interest as the building was faced with Carter's Architectural Tiles which were specially produced by Carter's Tiles of Poole. During the War it was thought at one period that on moonlit nights the reflection of the white frontage of the Regent was being used as a landmark by German aircraft crossing the coast en route to Bristol and the Midlands.

After the War no further effort was made by South Coast Theatres to proceed with plans made just before the War to construct a large new cinema on a site adjacent to the level crossing in the High Street.

The Regent continued to show films until 1968 when the final programme was GUESS WHO'S COMING TO DINNER starring Spencer Tracy and Katherine Hepburn on Saturday, 1 June.

Bingo continued at the Regent until 1977 when the cinema was finally closed and was demolished. The site was then incorporated into the Dolphin Centre and is now occupied by the Tesco supermarket and the Littlewoods store.

in 1980 an application for planning permission was made by Hope Enterprises Ltd to develop a Drive-in Cinema on a site at Canford Heath. Nothing further was heard of this proposal for a rather different type of cinema for Poole.

However, on 15 December 1989 U.C.I. opened their multi-million pound ten screen multiplex cinema at Tower Park on the southern edge of Canford Heath. Total seating is for 2000 patrons in ten separate auditoria. Comfortable seating, air conditioning and state of the art sound and projection systems are the order of the day here and there is always a wide choice of programme, including from time to time showings of classic films of earlier years.

The Arts Centre in Poole opened in 1978, incorporates a small well appointed cinema seating 109 in very comfortable style. There is the opportunity to see films here which are not always available elsewhere, although many of the quality current releases are also shown on a regular basis.

Regent, Poole prior to demolition 1977

U.C.I., Tower Park, Poole 1994

PORTLAND

Citizens of Portland were being offered film entertainment from about 1908. At Easton programmes were regularly presented in the Jubilee Hall prior to the conversion of the Methodist Chapel in Park Road into the Palace Cinema. Portland directory of 1915 shows that by this time Mr Albany Ward was the proprietor of the Palace. The building was of Portland stone and as a cinema it accommodated 298 patrons. Albany Ward ran a chain of mainly small cinemas in the West Country and the Channel Islands. The advertising of this cinema chain proudly proclaimed "Albany Ward's Imperial Electric Pictures - The Best in the West".

Old Palace Theatre, Easton

Originally power at the Palace was provided by a single cylinder gas engine driving a D.C. dynamo, and there was also a petrol driven back up plant. Subsequent proprietors were a Mr Hayes and Mr Waight until 1937 when Mr Les Weyman and Mr Eric Green in partnership became joint proprietors. Mr Weyman ran a radio

and electrical business in Easton, although in earlier years had started his working life with Albany Ward at the Palladium Cinema in Weymouth. During the Second World War projectionist Albert Chambers ran the Palace show virtually single handed.

Mr Emrys Stewkesbury who was involved as a projectionist at the Palace in post war years, recalls that in 1947 new projection equipment was installed followed by improvements to the auditorium. New suspended ceilings and improved lighting and stage curtains transformed the ambience of the cinema. Vista Vision and Cinemascope were installed around 1954. The Palace never opened on Sundays or showed any "H" category films, at least whilst in the ownership of Mr Weyman.

Old Mother Riley and George Formby epics and similar films were never shown at the Palace. If Easton people wanted Sunday entertainment or Old Mother Riley etc. they had to travel to the Regal at Fortuneswell or one of the Weymouth cinemas.

In 1971 Mr & Mrs Peter Warren of Weymouth remember seeing the film THE LAST PICTURE SHOW which related to events in a small American town cinema and its eventual closure.

Seeing this film made them remember their experience at the Palace Easton in 1958 when the film showing was THE ADMIRABLE CRICHTON.

The cashier informed them that they were the only customers except for one gentleman "left over from the first house". Eventually it was decided to proceed with the show despite the fact they were informed that the takings would not cover the cost of the carbons for the arc lamps. They were given the full programme with supporting film, travel feature and newsreel, and in the interval the ice cream girl attended upon them.

By the time the main feature film appeared they were the only people in the audience and were the sole witnesses of what was the "Last Picture Show" at the Palace, Easton.

After closure as a cinema the building became a youth club for some years before being demolished. The site is now occupied by residential property.

Masonic Hall, Victoria Square, Portland formerly Palace Cinema in 1920's

Albany Ward's cinema at Chiswell was the Palace which occupied the lower floor of the Masonic Hall in Victoria Square and according to a projectionist who recalls Portland cinemas during the 1920's had their own power supply and during flooding the engine was often under water, and seemed none the worse for it. The dynamo was apparently on an elevated platform and was not badly affected. The projection box was over the entrance hall and by all accounts very cramped indeed, access being by means of a vertical steel ladder.

Another Portland resident remembers being at a show in the Palace in the 1920's when the sea suddenly came over and the entire audience had to be ferried to safety in Queens Road. According to local people who attended shows at the Palace it appears that sound films were never presented and silent films were the order of the day. Musical accompaniment was provided by pianist Mr Bones or for special films by the Live Wires Dance Orchestra. The Palace closed in the early 1930's when the final programme was Greta Garbo in THE WOMAN OF AFFAIRS.

The Hayes family travelling repertory company showed films when visiting Portland on sites at Manger's Ground and Baker's Ground which was an old stone cutting yard. On the last visit to Chiswell the portable building became a fixture but to satisfy official requirements a concrete projection box had to be built. One local resident can recall seeing D W Griffiths's silent epic WAY DOWN EAST in the 1920's at the Bakers Ground cinema.

Local author and historian Mr Stuart Morris recalls that his father, Mr Frank Morris, and uncle, Mr Newton Morris, were very keen amateur projectionists during the 1920's and remember seeing their first stereoscopic films at the Palace, Chiswell. It appears that the projectionist had some difficulty with synchronising the projectors but the general impression was that the result was very effective. Mr Frank Morris bought the hand cranked Gaumont Paris projector from the old Palladium cinema at Town Bridge, Weymouth. Mr Newton Morris regularly presented children's film shows in the Brackenbury Church Hall - mainly comedies and Westerns, using a 16mm Wondertone projector.

The Regal, Fortuneswell which opened in 1932 was built for the Herbert family who were travelling showmen and well known in the area at this time. The new "Luxury Kinema" as it was billed, seated 562 patrons on one floor and was much welcomed by Portland people, according to press reports of the period.

Mr Bob Mutch, who was projectionist at the Regal in the years 1940-1944 and 1951-1961, recalls that the cinema roof was damaged by enemy action in 1941 and the Regal was closed for several weeks as a result. In 1940 the cinema was closed for a period when the manager Mr Reneff, left the Regal, and until the new manager, Mr Martin, was appointed there was no cinema entertainment in this part of Portland. During wartime days because of the popularity of films the Regal sometimes managed to squeeze in three programmes in an evening which could only be done by "cutting about" the programme to fit the bill.

In 1944 American servicemen would offer bribes to get a seat at the Regal, usually in the form of sweets and cigarettes which then of course were in very short supply.

In the 1950's a local consortium which included Les Weyman, proprietor of the Palace, Easton, took over the Regal and it remained in their ownership until closure as a cinema in 1961.

Subsequently the Regal reopened for bingo and a very occasional film. Eventually the building became a night club and in 1993 was badly damaged by fire.

The premises have now been virtually demolished and it appears that the site is to be redeveloped.

SHAFTESBURY

Some of the earliest memories of screen entertainment of any type in Shaftesbury are of magic lantern shows at the Ebenezer Hall in Salisbury Street, given by a Mr Pinney and his two sisters. These shows were mainly of an educational nature and were presented once a week.

It seems that the first actual film shows appeared in the town around 1914-1915 when the premises in High Street - now the Granada Television shop - were suitably adapted and became known as the Picture Palace.

Palace Cinema, Shaftesbury 1920's

American built "Optigraph" projector used in the original Palace Cinema, Shaftesbury

Life long resident of Shaftesbury, Mr Reg Humphries, recalls the magic lantern shows and the "moving pictures" at the Picture Palace, and even some of the films from the period just after the First World War.

Dramatic serials with a new exciting episode each week such as THE CAT CREEPS and DRACULA are still remembered by Mr Humphries with affection and amusement. Mr Phil Clements who in later years was a projectionist at the Savoy cinema remembers seeing Charlie Chaplin in THE CIRCUS at the Picture Palace.

In the mid 1920's the Picture Palace closed and the Market House in the upper part of the High Street was converted for use as a cinema and named the Palace. Mr Percy Coaker was the proprietor of the cinema this time. Phil Clements paints a vivid picture of an evening at the Palace. The projection room protruded into the foyer and access was by vertical wooden steps. There was no flue to clear the fumes from the carbon arc lamps so the "box" door was kept open when running - which was against regulations. The auditorium was notorious for its leaking roof resulting in frantic changes of seats in bad weather to avoid getting wet.

Although the films were silent there was plenty of general noise provided by the clatter of the projectors at one end of the hall and the pounding of the gas engines driving the generator at the other end. In addition to these "noises off" there was the pianist, Mr Gilbert Mitchell, providing musical accompaniment to the film programme. It appears that the audience consumed large quantities of peanuts and most of the empty shells found their way towards Mr Mitchell or his piano, and on occasions he refused to continue until this activity ceased and the piano was cleaned out.

The first "talkies" presented at the Palace in the late 1920's were "sound on disc". Due to the fact that many films were badly mutilated the sound was frequently "out of Sync" and breakdowns were not unusual. The first sound films at the Palace in 1930 was HIT THE DECK starring Jack Oakie. Mr Percy Carter was now the proprietor of the Palace and it seems that as early as 1929 plans existed for a new purpose built cinema for Shaftesbury.

The building and opening of the Savoy cinema in Bimport did not come about until 1933. The Savoy was designed in the stadium style with 380 seats by architect, Mr E de Wilde Holding, who was responsible for the design of several cinemas in Somerset, Dorset and Devon during this period. The builder of the Savoy was Ernest Boughton of Lychett Matravers, Dorset. There was some local opposition to the Bimport site as Shaftesbury's largest church was virtually opposite.

The first film at the Savoy was MAID OF THE MOUNTAINS starring Harry Welchman which was also the final programme at the Palace in the High Street.

Programmes at the Savoy in the 1930's were often augmented by variety shows provided by touring companies. Pantomimes were regularly staged by professional companies each January which entailed extra work for the projectionists. Phil Clements was a projectionists at the Savoy from 1936 until 1940 when he left for war service. He remembers that Mr Carter was very particular about the quality of all presentations and showmanship was very much the order of the day.

The ownership of the Savoy passed to Mr Elliott Turnbull in 1940. Mr Turnbull had been manager of the Regent, Bournemouth and prior to that manager of the New Gallery Cinema in London for the Gaumont British Picture Corporation. In the early 1960's Bassett Cinemas became the proprietors - they also owned the Plaza, Wincanton.

The Savoy celebrated its 50th anniversary in 1983 but in the following year closure was on the cards even though in the summer period of 1984 the most successful film ever screened at the Savoy did record breaking business for an extended period. The film in question was E.T. and according to Mrs Ann Stone, who managed the Savoy for Peter Lindsay Leisure in its final years, if that sort of business could have been maintained the Savoy might well have still been in operation today. The final film programme was CHAMPIONS starring John Hurt and Edward Woodward.

The local Film Society still present special programmes of films which are shown in the Old Market Playhouse in Shaftesbury, also known as the Arts Centre. These premises are in fact part of the building which constituted the Palace cinema of earlier years and some of the seats came from the Savoy, so there is this connection between the old and new silver screens of Shaftesbury.

Savoy Cinema, Shaftesbury 1934

Christmas at the Savoy 1980's

Demolition of the Savoy mid-1980's

SHERBORNE

Anderton and Rowland, the travelling showmen, presented animated picture shows at Sherborne Pack Monday Fairs from about 1906. Subsequently Mr A Coaker presented film shows at the Drill Hall and the Rawson Hall where seating was on planks across beer barrels. Mr Coaker also exhibited films at premises in Cheap Street where the furniture shop "Lancasters" now stands.

Mr Rowland Reeves who was involved with Mr Coaker, decided to build a new theatre at Newland. The new theatre was initially known as the Wessex and was opened by Lieutenant Colonel Wingfield Digby on 18 December 1929. Due to technical problems the first film was not shown until 20 December. The film was HUNGARIAN RHAPSODY.

The theatre was designed by Satchwell and Roberts of Birmingham. Seating 600 people its decor was described as being particularly striking with delicate colour schemes and tasteful lighting. Hand painted hunting and country scenes adorned the wall panels in the auditorium. Six dressing rooms were provided and the theatre was regularly used by local and travelling shows and on one occasion by a circus.

Within a year or so of opening the Wessex was taken over by Mr Percy Carter and Mr Pilkington who had full sound facility installed and renamed the theatre the Carlton. The name Carlton was derived from their surnames.

Mr Fred B Alcock, a leading member of the Sherborne Operatic and Dramatic Society, stated that the Carlton was "a gem of a theatre in every respect". Even so when they tried to get two grand pianos into the orchestra pit for a production of "No No Nanette" there was considerable difficulty.

Wartime days provided full houses at the Carlton, and staff who worked there with the then owner Mr Alan Seager, recall that they were busy and happy days. The Carlton closed on

Carlton Cinema, Sherborne closed 1961, main structure demolished 1989

2 February 1961 with the film THE PRIDE AND THE PASSION starring Cary Grant. The main structure remained until demolition in 1989 to make way for the supermarket. Some fittings were removed for use at the Plaza, Wincanton, which was being restored.

Several seats from the Carlton are displayed at Sherborne Museum.

SWANAGE

Prior to 1912 residents and holiday visitors in Swanage had to rely on the visits of travelling showmen in order to enjoy the films of the period.

The Swanage Town Guide of 1914 advertises "Up to date pictures well shown all the year round" at the Gilbert Hall Pictures in King's Road. This was the first cinema in Swanage and was opened in 1912 by the Southern Cinema Company, General Manager Mr D H Curtis.

Gilbert Hall, King's Road first cinema in Swanage

The hand cranked projectors were located in the gallery of the Gilbert Hall and were transferred to the newly built Electric Cinema in Station Road, which opened for business in June 1916. The Electric was built by local builder, George Pond. Gilbert Hall was then closed as a cinema but in later years was reopened for various types of entertainment under the name Purbeck Palace of Amusements (Unlimited). The owner of the 500 seat Electric, which became Swanage Cinema, was Mr F A Walton.

The operator/projectionist at Gilbert Hall was Mr Gerry Stockley who transferred to the new cinema.

The Cinema, Station Road, Swanage

In 1919 Mr Walton erected a wooden army hunt next to Swanage Cinema. The building was opened as Swanage Theatre but subsequently changed its name to Swanage Pavilion.

Alterations were carried out in 1920 and it eventually became known as the Grand Theatre. Swanage Times and Directory in November 1932 reported an application for a permanent cinematograph licence in respect of the Grand. The County Architect called for certain structural alterations before such a licence would be granted. It seems that the Grand commenced life as a cinema early in 1933.

Both cinemas were sold in 1936 to Portsmouth Town Cinemas. Until this Company took over very little advertising appeared in the local newspaper - Swanage Times and Directory.

The first front page display advertisement for the Cinema and the Grand appeared in the edition of 12 June 1936 under the banner of P.T.C. Programmes were TWO BLACK SHEEP starring Otto Kruger at the Cinema and NO MONKEY BUSINESS starring Rene Houston and Claude Dampier at the Grand.

The projection room at the Cinema was on the ground floor and if the projection room door was left open the noise of the projectors was very audible in the auditorium. At the Grand the projection room was on the roof and reached by an iron ladder which could be very hazardous especially when carrying reels of film in bad weather or during wartime blackout conditions. Projectionist, Mr Bob Dwen, who started as rewind boy in both cinemas in 1942, remembers the arrival of the American Army in Swanage during 1944. The Grand was showing a Betty Grable film which attracted packed houses afternoon and evening. In fact practically any film was well patronised at this period in Swanage, mainly due to the large numbers of Service personnel in the district. Press advertisements in the 1940's indicate that the Cinema opened all the year round but the Grand sometimes closed at the end of September and reopened again at the beginning of May for the summer season.

Despite the fact that Swanage suffered many enemy air attacks during the war years neither of the cinemas suffered major damage, although a high explosive delayed action bomb struck the front of the adjacent Railway Hotel during one raid. Fortunately, the bomb was dealt with promptly and caused only minor damage.

British actor, Leslie Banks, star of many classic films of the 1930's had a house in the village of Worth Matravers and was quite a regular patron of the cinemas at Swanage in the 1930's and 1940's.

Both cinemas continued to provide entertainment in the post war years as the numbers of visitors increased. In 1953 Portsmouth Town Cinemas sold both cinemas to Mr Tony Whitehouse. Mr Dick Mayo who had started work in the cinemas as a rewind boy in 1919 was managing both cinemas at this time.

Mr Whitehouse carried out considerable renovations and complete redecoration of both cinemas including reconstruction of the Grand's frontage and entrance hall. The Cinema at this time was renamed the Ritz.

Swanage Cinema in the 1930's and 40's

The Grand closed in November 1953. Final film programme on 7 November was ALWAYS A BRIDE starring Peggy Cummins and Ronald Reagan in LAW AND ORDER.

The following week Swanage Music Society presented MERRIE ENGLAND for four days. Somewhat appropriately the Ritz programme on 9th November was GONE WITH THE WIND. After alterations the Grand became the Ritz Ballroom.

The Ritz cinema continued until 3 October 1959 when the final film presentation was Yvonne Mitchell in SAPPHIRE and John Gregson in JACQUELINE.

The equipment and furnishings in the Ritz together with the contents of Lulworth Camp Cinema were auctioned at the Ritz on 7 October 1959. The Grand was eventually demolished and the site was redeveloped as the Gateway Supermarket and subsequently the Ritz building was incorporated into the same establishment.

Films are now shown regularly in the Mowlem Theatre which is equipped for full cinema presentations. Mr David Haysom, who is curator of the Tithe Barn Museum in Swanage and very enthusiastic about cinema entertainment, is actively involved with film shows at the Mowlem Theatre including duties as a projectionist.

WAREHAM

The Rex cinema at Wareham is unique in several respects. Film entertainment commenced here in 1920 and after approximately 75 years the town still enjoys nightly cinema performances.

The cinema which was originally known as the Empire, is unusual in that although many small towns started film shows in such premises and then moved on to purpose built theatres, Wareham's cinema remains as it started, with the auditorium occupying the upper floor of the Oddfellows Hall in West Street. The building was erected in 1889.

The Rex is certainly unique in Dorset and is probably a strong contender for being the oldest continuously operated independent cinema in the country.

Some older Wareham residents can recall seeing Rudolph Valentino in THE SHEIK and Charlie Chaplin in THE KID in 1921, and then in the late 1920's the excitement caused in the town by the arrival of the "talkies".

Over the years since 1920 there have been seven or eight proprietors including in the early thirties Mr Harry Mears who owned and managed many cinemas in the South of England, particularly in the Bournemouth area. Mr Mears became three times Mayor of Bournemouth and in the 1950's was President of the Cinematograph Exhibitors Association. Mr Cecil Elgar was the proprietor in

the mid-thirties, he was also the owner of the Palace Cinema at Freshwater on the Isle of Wight.

Mr Elgar was succeeded at the Empire by Mr Joseph Merrick who ran the cinema through the war years and until he was killed in a flying accident at Swanage in 1949. Mrs Violet Merrick continued to run the cinema for another fourteen years until 1963 when Mr Rusty Irons took over the management and it eventually became part of the Myles Byrne Cinema Group.

Towards the end of 1963 the cinema closed for refurbishment and reopened as the Rex on Boxing Day with the musical SOUTH PACIFIC. During the refurbishment Kalee '18' projectors (circa 1938) were installed which were originally in use at the Ritz, Blandford. In recent years the projectors have been changed again. They are still Kalee '18's but this pair came from a cinema that closed in Oxford in the 1980's and are matched with a veteran pair of President carbon arc lamps. In recent years the seating has been improved with equipment acquired from such diverse locations as the Finsbury Park Astoria and the Rio, Canvey Island. More recently seats were obtained from the Continental, Bournemouth when it closed in 1989. Currently the seating is for 151 patrons but originally the Empire seated 270.

During 'Rusty' Irons period of management there were a number of interesting events, not least when the Rex was the only cinema in Dorset to show LAST TANGO IN PARIS which ran every night for three weeks to full houses.

Mr Irons also recalls that when the film COMRADES, the story of the Tolpuddle Martyrs, was being filmed locally many of the "rushes" were first screened at the Rex, which was something a little different for a small market town cinema.

Empire Cinema, Wareham 1930's

Rex Cinema, West Street, Wareham 1990

When Mr Irons retired in 1987 management of the Rex passed to a group of local friends and enthusiasts who were determined that Wareham should not lose 'its' cinema. Since 1987 they have made great efforts and with the support of local people and a grant from the Purbeck Council they have managed to provide a variety of entertainment including special film festivals, all night horror programmes and foreign films usually only seen in specialist cinemas in the larger towns. Quite apart from films live entertainment has been offered from time to time, mainly featuring local talent.

Duties in the projection room are shared by a team of enthusiasts lead by chief projectionist, Dougal Dixon. Maintenance and repairs of the sound and projection equipment is ably taken care of by Ron Hickson who in earlier years had wide experience in the projection rooms of many of the leading cinemas in the Bournemouth and Poole area.

In January 1994 a special weekend Film Festival featuring the work of actor Alan Bates was held when many of his films were shown including FAR FROM THE MADDING CROWD, parts of which were filmed locally at Bloxworth House near Wareham. Alan Bates made a personal appearance on the Saturday evening to discuss informally his life and work as an actor.

The team who are successfully keeping the Rex in business have also added a cafe in premises which are a part of the original building and this now operates in conjunction with the cinema.

WEYMOUTH

The Southern Times of 30 January 1909 announced that Albany Ward's Imperial Electric Pictures would commence a grand picture season on 1 February in Weymouth's Jubilee Hall. Included in the programme was BLACK EYED SUSAN, and "wonderful pictures of the Terrible Earthquake" and other topical items.

Live entertainment was also included in the programme and this also applied to Weymouth Pavilion's presentation at this time which was advertised as a "Grand Display of the Latest Animated Pictures" with a programme of music by the Pavilion Orchestra.

Later the same month Albany Ward was presenting the latest improvement in talking and singing - The Cinephone, which was described as animated pictures and singing combined. Quite apart from his shows in the Jubilee Hall Albany Ward offered to attend any function with "The very latest machines - absolutely flickerless and fireproof, and fifty thousand feet of the latest films to select from".

In September 1909 Weymouth Municipal Band performances in the Alexandra Gardens and the Esplanade bandstand were supplemented with evening shows by The Walturdaw Cinematograph.

The next venture in cinema entertainment was by Albany Ward when he opened the Belle Vue Picture Palace on 5th December 1910 which according to press reports of the time was splendidly furnished and appointed throughout. During the opening performance there was frequent outbursts of applaused by a very enthusiastic audience. The first programme included such items as FONTOLINI STEALS A BICYCLE, SLEEPY SAM and a coloured epic entitled THE SHEPHERD'S KISS. Seating accommodation was similar in style to the one portrayed in the amusing British film of 1957, THE SMALLEST SHOW ON EARTH.

The next venue in Weymouth to offer films was when Mr Frederick Hall opened the Palladium Theatre at the Town Bridge on 29th July 1912. The original presentations at the Palladium were a mixture of theatrical shows and films. Advertisements for film shows at this period rather extravagantly claimed that "The Palladium comics are absolutely guaranteed to bring joy-tears to a pair of glass eyes."

Originally Palladium Cinema, Weymouth

During the 1920's the Jubilee Hall premises were known as the Royal Jubilee Hall and Opera House. The premises underwent a major rebuild and extension in 1926 and although the basic structure remained as before every effort was made to make the new Regent Theatre as modern and as comfortable as possible with provision for dancing in the attached Regent Dance Hall.

Opening day for the new theatre now in the ownership of Provincial Cinematograph Theatres was 2 August 1926 with total seating capacity of approximately 1400 including two boxes and a balcony lounge and cafe. Architect and designer was Mr W.E. Trent, F.S.I. and the main building contractors were Bartlett and Co. of Yeovil. The opening programme was a theatrical production entitled WELCOME HOME and the first feature

film presentation was on Sunday 8 August 1926 when PARISIAN NIGHTS was screened.

By the time "talkies" arrived in Weymouth in 1929 the Regent, Belle Vue and Palladium cinemas were all managed by Provincial Cinematograph Theatres Ltd. The Regent was the first to present "talkies" in the town and on 21st October 1929 BULDOG DRUMMOND starring Ronald Coleman was shown and advertised as "Direct from the Tivoli Theatre London". In the following year the Belle Vue was equipped for sound. Originally it was intended that sound equipment would be installed in the Palladium at Town Bridge but according to a Portland resident who was a projectionist in both cinemas during this period there was a sudden change of plan due to lack of space in the Palladium projection room which was apparently very cramped, even without the extra space required for the sound equipment.

The Palladium closed its doors finally on Saturday 3 January 1931. The last programme was LIFE'S LIKE THAT and PORT OF LOST SOULS.

The Gaumont British Company took control of the Regent and Belle Vue in the 1930's and the Belle Vue continued as Weymouth's second run cinema with the Rank Organisation until closure on Saturday 29 September 1956. When the Belle Vue closed Weymouth council considered purchasing the theatre for the use as a leisure centre including films but this idea did not materialise. The last programme at the Belle Vue was a double feature THE LYONS IN PARIS and INDIAN SCOUT starring George Montgomery.

The Pavilion or Pier Pavilion built in 1908 as the Pavilion Theatre provided film entertainment from the early 1930's until closed for war use in 1940. The Pavilion reopened in 1950 renamed the Ritz Theatre where films and live shows were presented until fire destroyed the buildings in April 1954.

Auditorium, Regent/Gaumont/Odeon in 1974

The Regent became the Gaumont in February 1951 and in subsequent years parts of the building became factory premises and later a night club. The Gaumont changed its name to the Odeon in September 1968 and eventually became The Top Rank Club, and continued as such until February 1976 when th Rank Organisation leased the premises to C.C.Leisure Ltd, who reopened the venue as the New Invicta Cinema and Bingo Hall on 8 February 1976.

Odeon, Weymouth 1971

After a long hot summer with poor support from the public the leisure company decided that it was no longer a viable proposition so the long association with entertainment of various types on this site ended on 29 January 1977 after nearly seventy years. The final programme was THE LANGUAGE OF LOVE and BLUE SEXTET.

One of the Kalee projectors from the New Invicta is now housed in the Tithe Barn Museum at Swanage where it is part of a reconstruction of a cinema projection room of the 1940's or 50's period.

Weymouth's sole surviving cinema at the time of writing in 1995 the Picturedrome in Gloucester Street has had a rather chequered history since its opening on 2 June 1933. The building was originally a stable complex which was part of the Gloucester Hotel and then became a bus garage for Rambler Motor Coaches which was a local company. Proprietor, Mr George Spivey, eventually disposed of the business to the Southern National Omnibus Company. Consideration was then given to the possibility of converting the building for use as a cinema.

Oscar Deutsch, founder and chairman of the Odeon Company was then involved with the project which became the second circuit Odeon but was rather modest in comparison to many of the later Odeon Theatres. The Picture House (Weymouth) Ltd. as the company was originally known, had as one of its local directors, Mr Spivey, although management of the theatre was administered by Mr Deutsch's head office in Birmingham.

The stadium style auditorium seated 541 and was originally decorated with murals which covered the entire length of both side walls. The first film presentation at the Odeon was LETTING IN THE SUNSHINE starring Albert Burdon. In 1967 the Odeon passed to Classic Cinemas which incorporated the Tatler Cinema Club in the 1970's who presented mainly 'X' certificate and uncensored film programmes.

Auditorium of Cannon Cinemas Weymouth 1993

Subsequently the Classic became part of the Cannon Cinema circuit and continued under their banner until January 1994 when Surrey based Picturedrome Theatres Ltd. became the new owners. This company also have cinemas at Chippenham, Bristol and Newport on the Isle of Wight.

The original Odeon of 1933 is now having a new lease of life as the Picturedrome. Refurbishment of the auditorium and improvements to the seating have been undertaken and a new Dolby sound system has been installed. Other improvements are planned so that Weymouths 412 seater cinema can continue to provide quality film entertainment for residents and visitors for many years to come.

Picturedrome, Gloucester Street, Weymouth 1994

WIMBORNE

One of the earliest recorded cinematograph entertainments in Wimborne was at a Conservative Club Fete at Eastbrook on 1 September 1909. The announcement in the Dorset County Chronical states that after a variety of events during the day "at dusk Mr A G Barralet will present a large cinematograph entertainment".

The Masonic Hall in the Cornmarket was also used for Bioscope film shows in those early years.

The Victoria Hall, which now forms part of the King's Head Hotel, was used for many types of functions including a cinema for many years, and continued to provide Wimborne's film entertainment well into the "talkie" era until the Tivoli came upon the scene in 1936.

Proprietor of the Victoria Hall cinema was local builder Mr A S Prince who also ran mobile cinema shows in Sturminster Marshall village hall and other village venues in the Wimborne district.

The Tivoli was built and owned by Mr Prince and was designed by Bournemouth based architect Mr E de Wilde-Holding LRIBA, who in the previous year or two had designed the Regal, Gillingham, Palace Blandford and the Savoy Shaftesbury. Chief assistant with the architect, Mr C H Fowler, recalls that there were qualms about the original designs for the Tivoli as the front of the proposed cinema was Borough House, a Georgian building of some importance. There was a large attractive garden with Georgian summer house at the rear including a fine ancient cedar tree which stood where the auditorium was built.

There was much excitement in the town on 24 August 1936 when film star, Jean Adrienne, arrived by train and then in a Rolls Royce to the Tivoli to declare the new cinema open. The first programme was FATHER O'FLYNN starring Jean Adrienne and Shirley Temple in KID IN HOLLYWOOD.

One unusual design feature was the lighting of the auditorium. Multi coloured concealed lighting gave a most attractive and pleasing effect of various colourings.

During the war business was very good at the Tivoli. On one occasion during this period the local Home Guard practising nearby fired a dummy mortar bomb into the roof of the cinema. Luckily it resulted in no major damage or injury.

In the early 1950's ownership of the Tivoli passed to South Coast Theatres Ltd but long serving manager, Mr Adams, continued to run the cinema. Subsequently, Myles Byrne Cinemas ran the Tivoli until its closure in April 1980 with the double feature programme CONVOY and SWEENEY 2.

Interestingly in the previous September there was an unusual presentation of films taken by Sir Alan Cobham on his pioneering flights in the 1920's and 1930's. Mr Michael Cobham made these long forgotten films available, and the special showings, which attracted much interest, were made in aid of Wimborne Squadron of the Air Training Corp.

Tivoli, Wimborne re-opened 1993

Ownership of the Tivoli site passed to the Dorset County Council and the building stood unused until 1990 when a group of enthusiasts led by former Wimborne Mayor and councillor, Mr Malcolm Angel, decided to form the Friends of the Tivoli and after 3 years really hard work and effort on 23 November 1993 Wimborne Festival Theatre Company presented ALPHABETICAL ORDER which really succeeded in bringing the Tivoli back to "life" again.

Restoration is by no means complete but a great deal has been accomplished with the aim in view that the Tivoli Theatre should become a multi purpose entertainment centre including full provision for the showing of films.

SILVER SCREENS FOR THE FORCES

Entertainment in some form was always considered a part of any large Service establishment and in this respect Dorset had its share of such activity.

Army, Navy and R.A.F. units provided cinema entertainment within the County, certainly from the time of the 1914-1918 war.

Bovington and Lulworth Camps

During the First World War cinema shows were being provided for Bovington's military personnel.

There was in fact two cinemas here in the early 1920's, one was built during the war and the other after the war. The earlier one became known as the Old Cinema and the later one was always the "Garrison" which seated about 500 patrons.

SKC Globe Cinema, Bovington Camp 1989

Mr Bill Bugg and his father were involved with the running of the Old Cinema in 1918 and in later years Mr Bugg was the proprietor of the Garrison Cinema and subsequently the new cinema which he had built opposite the Garrison in 1946. The new cinema continued under Mr Bugg's control until 1949 when it was acquired by the Army Kinema Corporation and became the Globe Cinema. Films have not been shown here for several years and the building is now used for storage purposes.

Mr Bugg's daughter can recall that when the family lived in premises which were part of the Garrison Cinema her bedroom backed on to the "screen wall" of the cinema and she could hear quite clearly the dialogue and music of the film being shown.

Another interesting wartime story from Mr Bugg's daughter concerns the film THE FIRST OF THE FEW which told the story of R J Mitchell the designer of the Spitfire.

It appears that for some reason the War Office wanted a special showing of the film prior to general release in 1942, and they chose Bovington's Garrison Cinema as the venue. Many high ranking military and government officials attended together with Leslie Howard the star of the film, accompanied by others responsible for the film's production. Personnel from nearby R.A.F. Warmwell were also invited to attend this unusual occasion.

Lulworth Camp did not have full cinema facilities but films were shown in the recreation hall on much the same pattern as at Bovington and were under Mr Bugg's control. It appears that shows continued until 1959 in this venue.

An auction announcement in the local press in October 1959 states that the contents of the Ritz Cinema, Swanage and Lulworth Camp cinema were to be sold by auction on 7 October 1959 including 35mm projectors which once were installed in the cinema aboard Cunard's "Queen Mary" ocean liner.

Blandford Camp

Cinema entertainment was available at Blandford Camp from the time of the First World War in several different locations. During the period 1939-1945 when there was considerable expansion of personnel on the camp including the location of the 22nd Group U.S. General Hospital H.Q. Cinema shows in and around Blandford were much in demand.

Writing in the U.S. Hospital Unit Magazine in September 1945 an American soldier patient complains bitterly that they would all like "much better movies on the base" and that it was "not much better in the village" (Blandford).

It appears that the U.S. authorities brought their own cinema with them but there was also an existing Garrison Cinema.

The Bournemouth Daily Echo reported in May 1964 that Blandford Camp was to be rebuilt with every modern amenity including a purpose built 300 seat cinema. The Army Kinema Corporation ran the new cinema for some years but films have not been shown on a regular basis in recent times although the building and its equipment are still intact.

Brownsea Island

During the Second World War considerable numbers of Service personnel were stationed on Brownsea Island in Poole Harbour. The island was also used as a transit unit for civilian and Service people.

Although facilities were rather limited there was a NAAFI canteen and ENSA provided live entertainment from time to time. There was also regular film shows which also appear to have been presented by ENSA in one of the recreational buildings on the island.

There is evidence that films were regularly ferried to Brownsea during this period and some local people recall actually being at film shows, but there is little information on where the "cinema" might have been.

Royal Navy – Portland

Exactly when cinema entertainment was first available on the Royal Navy establishment at Portland is difficult to ascertain but it seems that the building known as Building No. 23 was built on what was once known as H.M.S. Osprey during the Second World War when it was renamed H.M.S. Attack.

This building was fully equipped as a cinema but was also used for stage presentations and as a lecture theatre. Films were shown regularly until the mid 1980's but then it went the way of most Service cinemas and ceased operation, mainly due to the competition of television which was readily available on most Service units.

In 1992 an attempt was made to revive interest in cinema going at this venue but with little success.

ENSA Cinema adjacent to Portland Castle 1995

The gymnasium in the Fleet Club Building within the Naval base was also used as a cinema for some years and although the seating was not permanently in position the building was equipped with full projection room facilities.

During the Second World War another cinema was built to serve Royal Navy personnel at Portland. This cinema which is built in traditional small cinema style still stands opposite the Main administration block of the Royal Naval Air Station and adjacent to Portland Castle.

The reason it was built on this particular site was that in earlier years the present administration block was the Main canteen and Recreational Club and the present airfield was the Navy's Sports field.

The building ceased to operate as a cinema many years ago, certainly prior to 1968. It seems that cinema activities here in wartime days were run by ENSA, and later by the Royal Navy Film Corporation.

When it ceased to operate as a cinema it was used as a film store by the Royal Navy Film Corporation until a few years ago when the Army Kinema Corporation took over the supply and distribution of films to ships in commission.

Local Portland people can remember going to the cinema shows within the Royal Navy establishments and a variety of entertainments were enjoyed at these venues, particularly during the Second World War and in the early post war years.

Pantomimes for the youngsters were presented and variety shows were also on the bill from time to time.

R.A.F. Tarrant Rushton

The airfield was constructed in 1942 and on what was known as the domestic site near the main road to Blandford was the cinema which although basically a very large Nissen hut it had a high level projection room and seating for approximately 450 patrons.

During the peak of activity at Tarrant Rushton just prior to D-Day there was approximately 3000 Army and R.A.F personnel based here so the cinema was undoubtedly a very useful amenity.

In 1945 many returning British Prisoners of War were in transit through Tarrant Rushton and no doubt they also appreciated the opportunity to go to the cinema again.

The site was cleared many years ago but interestingly until the 1960's one wall of the building remained with the projection room "port holes" clearly visible.

Wareham (Worgret)

During the First World War a large army camp existed at Worgret to the West of the town.

Included in what was said to be one of the finest army camps in England was a garrison cinema to cater for the entertainment of about 7000 men who were stationed there.

Local people were permitted to attend these film shows. After the war the camp was dispersed and local people eventually found themselves enjoying films at the Empire in West Street which began its life as a cinema in 1920.

Garrison Theatre, Worgret, Wareham

R.A.F. Warmwell

The cinema building still exists here and continues to serve a very useful purpose - namely the village hall for the Crossways village community.

According to Major General H.M.G. Bond who now owns the building, it was constructed as a cinema and for general recreational use after a Luftwaffe raid in August 1940 on this Battle of Britain airfield. The raid caused extensive damage to living quarters and other facilities and casualties to R.A.F. personnel on the operational

Originally Station Cinema R.A.F. Warmwell

site. As a result the existing building is quite isolated from what was once the airfield.

When the building was functioning as a cinema during the 1940's local people were allowed admission subject to the discretion of R.A.F. authorities.

The field in which the cinema village hall stands has been known locally as the "Cinema Field" since the 1940's.

During the period 1939-1945 when there were Service units located throughout the County efforts were made to provide entertainment for personnel even those in small units in the remote corners of Dorset. ENSA provided travelling live shows and had some involvement with mobile cinema outfits but in the early war years equipment was in very short supply, especially good quality 16mm projectors, which were eventually obtained from the United States, but then there were difficulties with spares for these machines. The ENSA mobile cinema units visited even the smallest units such as the anti-aircraft gun sites and searchlight detachments, of which there were many especially in the coastal areas.

The R.A.F. Station at Worth Matravers near Swanage was typical of the medium size units visited by ENSA, but the larger establishments such as Bovington, Portland and the R.A.F. Stations had their own permanent cinemas, as has already been mentioned.

The film division of ENSA was known as FENSA - Film Entertainment National Service Association - and was devoted to obtaining the best possible films for Service audiences, wherever they happened to be. This was sometimes not at all easy as they had to cope with restrictions such as an agreement with the Cinematograph Exhibitor's Association not to show films within a two miles radius of any commercial cinema, and there were difficulties getting up to date films, particularly when it came to 16mm versions of popular films.

However, in Dorset this was not usually a serious problem as cinemas were relatively few and far between so there was seldom any serious competition for the Service audiences. Some units such as the anti-aircraft site at Hurn - now Christchurch Sports Club - had a permanent cinema in one of the recreational buildings. This was used by R.A.F. and U.S.A.A.F. personnel based at the R.A.F. Station at Hurn.

The American Army Hospital at St. Leonards also had cinema facilities but it is now known if this was a purpose built cinema or a suitable building temporarily adapted.

In the North of the County at Yetminster local farmer Mr Jack Partridge recalls the influx of Service personnel in and around the village during the Second World War. Units from the Royal Ulster Rifles and the Sussex Regiment were amongst those who were stationed in the village and utilised the Church Hall and the Vicarage for accommodation and recreational purposes. Film shows were provided in the village hall by ENSA and local people were admitted if there was enough room. Mr Partridge remembers seeing the 1939 version of THE HOUND OF THE BASKER-VILLES as a member of a very crowded audience packed into the Church Hall one cold winter night in the early 1940's.

Residents in Cranborne in the War years can remember regular film shows in a section of the old village hall which was used as a NAAFI canteen by a unit of the Royal Artillery (Search-light) Regiment who were based at The Lodge, Cranborne at this time.

Most of the sites relating to military operations during the Second World War have disappeared completely with the exception of establishments such as Blandford, Bovington, Lulworth and Portland.

It will probably never be known exactly where, when or how film entertainment was provided for all the Service units that existed in Dorset during those years but hopefully a broad outline and flavour of such activities has been covered in these paragraphs.

CINEMAS IN THE COUNTRYSIDE

The West Country Showmen Anderton and Rowland, who visited Sherborne Pack Monday Fair with their No.1 Bioscope Show in the early years of this century, were responsible for bringing the first film entertainment to the smaller communities and villages of Dorset. Reports from this period show that Anderton and Rowland used lions to attract customers to their Bioscope Shows when touring the West Country. Apart from these fairground shows other rural cinema entrepreneurs were bringing the silver screens to the villages.

The Bere Regis parish magazine of 1903 reported that a film show was given by a Mr Baker of Salisbury. Included in the programme was a film of the 1902 Coronation of Edward VII. It seems very likely that these shows took place in the Drax Hall, Bere Regis, which celebrated its centenary in 1994 and has been used for most village activities during its lifetime. Another venue used in the 1930's and 1940's and recalled by local author Mr Fred Pitfield, was the old Women's Institute hut at Southbrook where the Bailey Brothers of Winterborne Kingston presented regular film shows.

After the Second World War weekly shows were given in the Drax Hall. According to Mr Pitfield the films were by no means up to date but were usually of good quality and featured such classics as OH MR PORTER, THE WICKED LADY and DR JEKYLL AND MR HYDE.

It seems many residents of Bere Regis particularly at weekends would visit the larger town cinemas such as the Regent, Poole and the Palace and Plaza in Dorchester. Transport was always a problem as bus services were sparse and inconveniently timed, and car ownership was by no means as commonplace as in later years.

Sturminster Newton enjoyed film shows from the early 1920's in The Hut which is now part of the British Legion Hall. North Dorset mobile cinema operator Mr Charlie Walford presented these shows on a weekly basis, assisted by Miss Inkpen on the piano.

Drax Hall, Bere Regis

Mr Max Harvey of Sturminster Newton relates that he assisted Mr Walford with the projection equipment and collecting ticket money at the door. He also recalls that Mr Walford's transport was a Model T Ford car and on one occasion in the 1920's he dismantled the engine and replaced the "big end" and the car was ready to leave at the end of the show with all the equipment aboard. Some residents of Sturminster Newton can still recall how basic and uncomfortable The Hut really was in those days. One regular film fan remembers that it was necessary to wear flying boots or similar in winter to keep out the cold air that came through the gaps in the flooring.

The Hut, Bath Road, Sturminster Newton

Another operator by the name of Jeans took over the business and this resulted in a permanent tin hut being erected to accommodate the projectors and electrical equipment adjacent to The Hut.

In the years immediately before and during the Second World War local Methodist minister, the Reverend Eva, ran a mobile cinema unit which provided regular entertainment at Sturminster Newton, Stalbridge and other Blackmore Vale villages.

At Stalbridge the village hall, which in the 1930's was also known as The Hut, was the venue for film shows from the time of the First World War. Stalbridge residents can remember the crowded smoke filled hall where they first saw the stars of the 1930's and 1940's. These shows must have been popular as there was always two performances on the weekly visit of the cinema to The Hut.

At Sixpenny Handley local men, Gordon Clarke and Edwin Froud ran film shows in the old village hall during the Second World War and they provided similar shows at Wimborne St Giles, the Gussages and other villages in this part of Dorset.

The Poole and East Dorset Herald in September 1921 reported that the Wessex Mobile Electric Cinema, who mainly operated in the East Dorset villages, had their Towers No 6 Cameragraph projector stolen from their lorry whilst enroute from Kinson to West Moors for an evening show at Cranborne. The show was cancelled that night but the thief was caught and duly appeared at Dorset Assizes.

Mobile cinema units visited Cerne Abbas between the wars and during the 1940's and 1950's. Local man, Mr Charlie Cornick, provided regular shows in the village hall. Patrons at Cerne's "cinema" seem to recall that Laurel and Hardy feature films and Westerns were almost always included in these programmes and were very enthusiastically received.

Some residents of Cerne Abbas can recall in the 1930's and 40's a farmer at the nearby village of Sydling St Nicholas establishing a small cinema in a barn. It appears that the projection and seating equipment was a permanent set up and regular film shows were provided and patronised by residents of Cerne Abbas and the surrounding villages.

In the Beaminster area mobile cinemas provided shows in many villages including Broadwindsor, Maiden Newton, Evershot, Cattistock, Winsham and Netherbury. Garage proprietor, Mr Frank Bridle of Beaminster provided film shows during the 1930's in this part of West Dorset.

Mr Ken Payne of Mosterton who was much involved with mobile cinemas recalls that in addition to the shows in halls and similar venues, open air shows were quite common using large custom built motor vans. These vehicles had a self contained generator and the projector mounted in the van body focussed on a rear view translucent screen with suitable masking. Shows with these vans were usually of films from the Ministry of Information or similar official sources and National Savings campaigns etc. Many of the wartime Crown Film Unit productions were shown in these cinema vans which travelled the country during the Second World War.

Mr and Mrs Payne ran film shows on a regular basis mainly in West Dorset and parts of Devon and Somerset in the 1940's, 50's and 1960's. They were particularly involved with shows at the Public Hall at Beaminster which was a better venue in respect of accommodation and the fact that the projectors could be housed in a projection room which isolated the machines from the audience. An old "Magic" lantern was used to show slides of forthcoming programmes and sweets and soft drinks were sold during the show.

Mr Felix Simmons of Bridport was also very active in running mobile shows in the Beaminster and Bridport localities. He had a reputation of being a first-class showman and lit the front of every hall with bright signs announcing the names of the films and "Cinema Tonight - Doors open at 7 start 7.30".

Herbert's, the funfair proprietors of Dorchester, entered the mobile cinema field in putting on shows at a public house in Maiden Newton but apparently this enterprise did not prove to be very successful.

These patterns of cinema entertainment were typical in most rural areas and the weekly or bi-weekly visits to these venues were very much a regular part of life in many of Dorset's smaller communities. It would not be possible to list all such places and activities but hopefully the foregoing gives some general idea and flavour of rural film entertainment in the County in the first half of this century.

More recently in 1976 a scheme was initiated by Dorset Community Council offering village hall block booking rates for selected films. This was due to a request from village communities for information on how to provide films of good quality in isolated areas.

Eventually twenty village halls throughout the County took part in the scheme with a collective audience of about 2000. One of the most successful village shows was at Corfe Castle where live shows of various types were combined with the films, which sometimes included films made by local people.

It appears that these shows were very well organised by the village hall teams at Corfe Castle and the "Picture Palace" shows were

Mobile 3D Cinema

popular and well supported in the late 1970's and early 1980's.

Travelling showmen were mentioned at the start of this section on mobile shows and it is interesting to note that in the 1990's there is still occasionally film entertainment of this type to be seen. The Great Dorset Steam Fair at Tarrant Hinton in recent years has included a very modernistic 3D mobile cinema. In comparison to the Bioscope shows of ninety years ago it was very large and sophisticated but both caused interest and amusement in their time and both entertained by means of a projected picture.

THEATRE ORGANS AND ORGANISTS

In any review of cinemas in Dorset mention must be made of the theatre organists and their instruments, who were once a part of any programme in the larger cinemas.

Electric Theatre, Commercial Road, Bournemouth

The Christie organ was installed when the Electric was equipped for sound and refurbished in 1930. This organ was said to be the only such instrument fitted with "Radiotone" which was said to increase its versatility.

Many organists appeared at the console over the years including:- Frank Matthew - "direct from the New Gallery, London" (1930), Alex Taylor (1931), Reginald Stone, Jack Courtenay, Paul Gomez, Jack Bath, Elton Roberts, and Reginald Hayward.

The organ was in use until 1954 when it was considered to be beyond repair, mainly due to the effects of a severe woodworm attack on some of the components. Subsequently it was removed and disposed of as scrap, although some items were made available to a theatre organ enthusiasts organisation.

Regent Theatre, Westover Road, Bournemouth (later The Gaumont)

The Wurlitzer organ was installed when the Regent opened in 1929. The organist for the first programme and for some months subsequently was Reginald Foort who was a leading theatre organist at this time. He was assisted by Phil Park on the Wurlitzer and as a pianist.

In later years organists appearing at the Regent included:- Kevin Buckley (1930), Kenneth Bygott (1936), Terence Casey, Lloyd Lewis, Harold Ramsay, Jack Bath and Ronald Brickell. Other instrumentalists included pianists Edith Buckley and Alex Haddow.

Special mention must be made of local musician Ronald Brickell who held the position of resident organist and house manager at the Regent for 25 years commencing in 1940.

MR. ALEX F. TAYLOR

The Man who makes the Majestic Christie Organ more majestic at Bournemouth Electric Theatre. Audience agree no "stops" required when he is playing. The picture accompanist complete and then some. Can make the Silent Screen talk and the Talkie Screen talk more. Made a reputation in two Continents. America still shouting: "Come back, kid." But America doesn't know Bournemouth. Alex. F. T. does Good for Bournemouth

Alex F. Taylor

Ronald Brickell

After starting his professional musical career as pianist with a trio in W H Smith's Old English Tea Rooms in Bournemouth in the early 1930's he trained as a theatre organist in various local theatres and in 1936 joined the Gaumont British Company in London. Initially he was organist at the Dominion Tottenham Court Road and later the Marble Arch Pavilion and the New Victoria. He became resident organist at the prestigious Gaumont in the Haymarket until the outbreak of war when he returned to Bournemouth and in 1940 was appointed resident organist at the Regent.

Thus began his long association with this theatre which included a wide variety of musical presentations during the war years including many B.B.C. broadcasts for the Forces Overseas programmes, which were live broadcasts transmitted at six or seven o'clock in the morning. Special musical programmes after normal cinema hours on Sunday nights were given for the large numbers of Royal Canadian Air Force personnel who were stationed in the town.

The Regent's 19th anniversary presentation in 1948 which included organists Terence Casey, Louis Mordish, Bobby Pagan and Ronald Brickell was by all accounts a major success. During the 1950's a radio programme entitled "SEASIDE NIGHTS" featured dual broadcasts from the Regent and its near neighbour the Westover with Eric Spruce at the Compton organ.

Ronald Brickell featured in a regular weekly B.B.C. programme covering the years 1945-1958. "MELODY FOR LATE EVENING" presented the theatre organ together with violin and voice. Local violinist Harold C Gee and tenor Francis Pope were often the artists concerned.

Prior to the "twinning" of the Gaumont in 1968 the Wurlitzer was removed to an organ collector's museum near Looe in Cornwall and in later years was found a new home in Alberta, Canada.

In 1958 when the Odeon (Lansdowne) was showing "SOUTH PACIFIC" for a season an electronic organ was installed and played daily by Ronald Brickell to enhance the presentation.

Jack Bath who appeared at the console of most theatre organs in this area began his musical career at St. Paul's Church, Bournemouth. He played the piano at the original Electric Cinema in Bournemouth from the time of the First World War. Subsequently he studied the theatre organ under Kevin Buckley at the Regent, Bournemouth (later the Gaumont). He joined the Gaumont British Company at the Tivoli, London and was organist at many of the leading thatres, including the Dominion, Tottenham Court Road. The A.B.C Forum at Southampton was a cinema

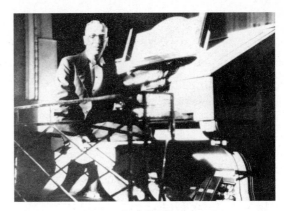

Jack Bath

that he was also much associated with over the years. He also spent four years on Cunard's "Queen Mary" as resident organist.

Astoria Cinema, Christchurch Road, Boscombe

The Astoria theatre organ at the Astoria was in regular use during the 1930's and 1940's. It appears that Melbourne Holman, Leslie Lawrence, Reginald O. Hanson and Johnson Lewis were among the regular organists who entertained at this cinema.

Westover Cinema, Westover Road, Bournemouth

Reginald Porter-Brown was at the console of the Compton organ when the Westover opened on 19 June 1937. Included among subsequent organists were the following:- Harold Coombs, Eric Spruce (1946) Reginald New (1946), Elise Granados (1946).

Eric Spruce and Reginald Porter-Brown were regular guest organists at the Westover over many years.

Coronation Cinema, Holdenhurst Road, Bournemouth

It appears that there was an orchestral pipe organ installed in the Coronation (later the Roxy) but little is known concerning its use over the years.

Regent Theatre, High Street, Poole

When the Regent opened in 1926 a three manual organ was installed.

In 1931 it was replaced by a new Christie organ designed especially for this theatre and from that time until its removal in 1968 many organists performed on what was the only permanent theatre organ in a Dorset cinema, Bournemouth not then being in the County.

Organists at the Regent included:- Jack Taylor (1931), Derek Ronald (1932), Alex Taylor, Herbert Maxwell (1932), Frederick Schofield (1938), Herbert Marshall - "direct from Paramount Theatre, Newcastle-on-Tyne" (1939), Derek Rowe, Archie Newman, Harry Farmer, Art Jenkins, Howard Jennings, Jack Bath, George Senior - first broadcast of organ (1946), Elton Roberts and Reginald Hayward.

The organ was little used after the late 1950's and in 1968 it was removed and eventually installed in the ballroom of the Antelope Hotel, Poole where regular concerts were given by guest organists.

After six years at the Antelope Hotel the Christie organ was moved to a new location in the Woodlands Court Ballroom on the Sandford Park Holiday complex near Wareham.

The installation has been very skillfully carried out and included an organ lift so that the Christie rises on to the stage in much the same way as it did in earlier years at the Regent.

Brian Sharp with the Regent Christie organ at Sandford Park

Reginald Hayward

CINEMA INDEX

BIBLIOGRAPHY

BRITISH FILM INSTITUTE FILM AND TELEVISION HANDBOOKS (Various)
BOVINGTON TANKS - George and Anne Forty
HALLIWELL'S FILM GUIDE
HALLIWELL'S FILMGOER'S COMPANION
KELLY'S DIRECTORIES (Various)
KINE YEAR BOOKS (Various)
REMINISCENCES OF THE CINEMA IN BOURNEMOUTH - Eric A George